Larry & Ru

The New Christian Traveler's Guide to the Holy Land

The New Christian Traveler's Guide to the Holy Land

Charles H. Dyer and Gregory A. Hatteberg

Moody Publishers
CHICAGO

Cover Design by Paetzold Associates
Cover Photos by Tim Dowley, with the exception of
Wailing Wall and Dome of the Rock by Corbus
Photos inside the book were supplied by the authors
Interior Design by Ragont Design
Edited by Jim Vincent

Library of Congress Cataloging-in-Publication Data

Dyer, Charles H., 1952-
The new Christian traveler's guide to the Holy Land / Charles H. Dyer and Gregory A. Hatteberg.
p. cm.
Revised and enlarged edition of: The Christian traveler's guide to the Holy Land.
Includes bibliographical references.
ISBN-10: 0-8024-6650-8
ISBN-13: 978-0-8024-6650-1
1. Israel—Guidebooks. 2. West Bank—Guidebooks. 3. Egypt—Guidebooks. 4. Greece—Guidebooks. 5. Turkey—Guidebooks. 6. Bible—Geography. 7. Christian pilgrims and pilgrimages—Israel—Guidebooks. I. Hatteberg, Greg, 1957- II. Dyer, Charles H., 1952- Christian traveler's guide to the Holy Land. III. Title.

DS103.D943 2006
915.604'5402427—dc22

2005024934

We hope you enjoy this book from Moody Publishers. Our goal is to provide high-quality, thought-provoking books and products that connect truth to your real needs and challenges. For more information on other books and products written and produced from a biblical perspective, go to www.moodypublishers.com or write to:

Moody Publishers
820 N. LaSalle Boulevard
Chicago, IL 60610

7 9 10 8

Printed in the United States of America

This book is lovingly dedicated to our wives,
Kathy Dyer and Lisa Hatteberg,
who share our love for the lands of the Bible.

"Many women do noble things, but you surpass them all."
PROVERBS 31:29

ONTENTS

C O N T E N T S

C O N T E N T S

C O N T E N T S

Introduction

Knowing the land of the Bible is as important to understanding God's Word as knowing the layout of a baseball diamond is to comprehending the game of baseball! Imagine explaining a baseball game to a friend from another culture who had never seen, or played, the sport.

You casually mention the baseball diamond, and your listener pictures a small stone dangling from a necklace. You excitedly describe a close play at second base while your friend wonders how many bases the ball controls . . . and if the "bases" are heavily guarded. You cheer when the manager summons the ace reliever from the bull pen while your bewildered companion envisions a victorious matador striding from a pen of bulls.

You may smile at the analogy, but we all do something similar when we read the Bible. We hear the story of Gideon choosing his three hundred men by the spring of Harod, and we substitute our own image of the event. Some picture a small stream thirty feet wide, while others see a broad river hundreds of feet across. Some imagine the water rushing down a steep mountainside, while others envision it meandering across flat plains.

The problem is that in many cases our own images cloud the biblical account and make it harder to understand. What makes perfect sense to someone standing at the spot where it happened seems almost incomprehensible to someone who has never been to the Holy Land and who reads the account knowing only the geography of Pennsylvania, Illinois, or Texas.

Traveling to Israel helps an individual view the Bible through a new set of geographical lenses. Simple phrases like "going up to Jerusalem" jump off the pages of God's Word because they now make sense. Capernaum becomes more than just a name on a page. Israel's temptation in the wilderness comes alive when your feet stumble over the desert rocks and your water bottle starts to run dry.

God chose this land to teach His people specific lessons of faith.

But why would God select for His people a land of marginal climate that was coveted by larger surrounding nations?

Jim Monson has offered a provocative explanation for God's choice. "In all of these biblical periods this land served as God's testing ground of faith. It was here, in this land where both personal and national existence were threatened, that Israel's leaders and people were called upon to learn the true meaning of security and well-being, of trust in the Lord their God. It was here that God's weakness was shown to be stronger than men" (James M. Monson, *The Land Between: A Regional Study Guide to the Land of the Bible* [Jerusalem: n.p., 1983], 14).

If you are reading this book in preparation for a trip to the Middle East, congratulations! You are about to take a journey that will make a profound spiritual impact on your life. You will soon traverse a region where God actively intervened in the lives of men and women . . . where the incarnate Son of God taught, healed, died for your sins, and rose from the dead. You will return a different person. This expanded edition of *The Christian Traveler's Guide* will also let you prepare for visits to other regions of the Holy Land: Egypt, Greece, Jordan, and Turkey.

We suggest you read part 1, "Preparing for the Trip," as soon as possible. In that section we offer specific information to help you prepare physically and spiritually for this journey of a lifetime. Once you know your final itinerary, begin reading the information on the specific sites you will visit. This will prepare you to gain as much information as possible from your trip. During your tour, keep this book with you as a handy guide . . . and as a convenient place to take notes, record pictures, and write your impressions. These records will be invaluable to you as you return home.

Our prayer for you is that this journey to the places of the Bible will make as profound an impact on your life as it has made on ours. Go with an open, receptive heart and ask God to give you a sense of wonderment, awe, and excitement as you "walk through the length and breadth of the land" (Gen. 13:17).

Charlie Dyer
Sun City West, Arizona

Greg Hatteberg
Dallas, Texas

PART ONE

Preparing for the Trip

- Travel Safety Facts
- Tips for Travelers
- Packing List
- Requirements for Obtaining a U.S. Passport
- How to Overcome Jet Lag
- Helpful Web Sites
- A Four-Week Schedule of Bible Reading and Prayer
    - —To Prepare for Israel
    - —To Prepare for Egypt and Jordan
    - —To Prepare for Greece and Turkey
- A Four-Week Bible Series to Prepare a Group Spiritually for a Trip to Israel

TRAVEL SAFETY FACTS

1. Airport security for all flights to the Middle East is very thorough.

2. Terrorist incidents in those Middle East countries visited by tourists, though well publicized in the media, are extremely rare.

3. There is more danger of death or injury driving from one's home to the airport than of being attacked by terrorists while on tour.

4. The governments of Israel, Egypt, Greece, Jordan, and Turkey take the safety of tourists very seriously and have implemented extraordinary measures in the past several years to increase security.

5. Several steps can be taken to minimize even further one's chances of being involved in terrorist incidents.

    - Keep a low profile. Try not to be conspicuous in your dress, speech, or behavior.
    - Avoid wearing articles of clothing that advertise your nationality or that actively identify you with one side or the other in the current Middle East conflict.
    - Avoid crowds, protest groups, or other potentially volatile situations that could present safety or security risks.
    - Stay with your group and avoid wandering off alone (similar to the advice you would give someone coming to visit any major city in the United States).
    - Dress and act in a manner that shows proper respect for the social and cultural values of the region. Avoid falling into the "Ugly American" stereotype.
    - Remain aware of your circumstances and surroundings. Don't become so absorbed by the grandeur of the sites that you fail to keep track of what is happening around you. If

you sense anything out of the ordinary, don't hesitate to express your concerns to the tour guide or tour leader.

6. Tour buses are in constant contact with their headquarters. The tour operators monitor any potential trouble spots; and if they feel there might be a problem, they will contact the guide and driver and reroute the group to avoid the area.

TIPS FOR TRAVELERS

Clothing

Most tours to the Middle East are very informal. (No real dress-up occasions, even for Sunday.) For touring, plan to wear comfortable clothes. Most tours encourage participants to wear jeans or slacks on the trip. Take one jacket or heavy sweater, even during the summer months. Remember when packing: Less is better. Comfortable shoes with nonskid soles are necessary. (You will be doing a great deal of walking, often over uneven terrain and smooth stone.) Wash-and-wear items are very helpful, and shorts are acceptable. However, those who wear shorts should also carry a "modesty kit" for visiting holy sites or traveling in more conservative areas so that knees and shoulders are covered. A modesty kit for women should include slacks or a wraparound skirt (below the knee) and a blouse that covers the shoulders. A modesty kit for men should include long pants, a shirt that covers the shoulders, and a hat.

Currency

Depending on what is covered in your tour, extra expenses may include incidental food items (beverages, snacks, lunch, etc.). You will also want to bring money to purchase souvenirs. Of that amount, you should carry $50 in $1 bills with the rest in cash or U.S. traveler's checks. (The $1 bills can be used to purchase bottled water, soft drinks, postcards, etc.) Should you need to do so, you can exchange dollars into the local currency at airports, hotels, and banks. Whenever you exchange dollars, keep the receipt given to you. You will then be able to convert any remaining currency back into dollars when you leave the country. Most stores love U.S. dollars, but you can sometimes get better bargains if you pay in the local currency.

The basic unit of money in each country is as follows:

- Israel uses the New Israeli Shekel (NIS), which is divided into 100 Agorot.
- Egypt uses the Egyptian Pound (£E), which is divided into 100 Piastres.
- Greece uses the Euro (€), which is divided into 100 Cents.
- Jordan uses the Jordanian Dinar (JD), which is divided into 100 Piastres.
- Turkey uses the New Turkish Lira (YTL), which is divided into 100 Kurus.

Just before leaving on your trip, check the Foreign Currency Exchange section in your local newspaper to determine the current exchange rate, or check the rate online at
http://www.oanda.com/convert/classic

You should consider the use of a money belt. Clever pickpockets are waiting for you. Carry and guard your passport, pocketbook, purse, and other valuables very carefully. Keep your money, traveler's checks, and passport on your person or in your hotel safe-deposit box. Never pack them in your suitcase or leave them in your hotel room. Larger purchases can be made using a major credit card (except the Discover Card), but go through your wallet or purse before leaving the United States to remove all unnecessary credit cards (just in case your wallet is lost or stolen).

Electric Appliances

The electric current in the different countries of the Middle East is 220-volt AC, single phase, 50 cycles, which requires special adapter plugs that can vary by country. If you intend to take appliances (hair dryer, electric razor, iron) that are suitable for both 110 and 220 volts, make sure to carry a set of adapter plugs. If your appliance is for 110 volts only, you will also need a converter. Never plug a 110-volt appliance into a 220-volt outlet without a converter; it will work at twice its speed for a few seconds—and never work again!

Health

No shots or vaccinations are required to visit most tourist destinations in Israel, Egypt, Greece, Jordan, or Turkey. However, you might want to visit the Centers for Disease Control and Prevention Web site to learn about illnesses specific to these countries and how best to protect yourself (**http://www.cdc.gov/travel**). Should you need medication during the trip, be sure to carry it with you. Also, take some of the following items along for any emergencies: Pepto Bismol (liquid or tablets), Imodium, sleeping pills (to help overcome jet lag the first few nights), Dramamine (if you are subject to motion sickness), cold or allergy tablets (if you are subject to allergy attacks), and any other personal hygiene products you may require.

Luggage

International airlines normally limit passengers to one suitcase and one carry-on bag (excluding purse or camera bag). In addition to satisfying airline regulations, this limitation also makes it much easier for individuals to keep track of their luggage when it is being loaded and unloaded from the buses and when it is portered at hotels. Be sure your suitcase closes and fastens securely (use extra straps if necessary). Mark your suitcase and carry-on bag clearly so you will be able to distinguish it. Women should consider using only their initials rather than their first name. Do not pack cameras, expensive jewelry, or other valuables in your suitcase.

Current airline security regulations require that checked baggage be unlocked. However, there are now locks available that are Transportation Security Administration (TSA) approved. These locks can be opened by the TSA and then relocked. Consider buying a set of TSA-approved locks if you wish to lock your luggage.

Be sure to have anything you will need while flying in your carry-on bag. Also keep your essential toiletries and a one-day change of clothes with you in your carry-on luggage (just in case your baggage would get "lost in transit"). Don't overpack. Leave some room for items you may purchase and bring back. Remember that on the way over you will be wearing the same clothes for two days—walking, riding, and sleeping in airplanes. Dress for comfort!

Meals

Hotels usually serve nutritious breakfasts, so don't skip breakfast! Lunches may or may not be included in your tour. (Check your travel brochure.) Dinner will be ample. Some foods will be new to you. Any foods served at the hotels will usually be safe to eat. Exercise care in eating unpeeled fruit and fresh vegetables purchased in open-air markets unless you peel and/or wash them first. Consider bringing along some snack foods to eat on the bus when you are traveling.

While the tap water in most hotels is usually safe, if you have any doubts, consider purchasing and drinking bottled water. Coffee, tea, and soft drinks are also safe to drink. Depending on the specific country and locale, you might need to exercise care about using ice. Plan to pay for any extra drinks you order for meals. (These are not usually included in the price of a tour.)

Other Items to Pack

Consider packing moist towelettes for warm touring days, and a washcloth—if needed—since some hotels do not supply them. Bring your own soap if it is important to you. Don't forget your sunglasses, and remember that a hat is an absolute necessity. (One with a broad brim is a wise choice.) You can request a wake-up call from most hotels, but you may also want to carry your own alarm clock. Boxed snacks (dried fruit, etc.) can help keep one's energy up between meals. Any liquids you take should be in tight (preferably plastic) bottles. Only fill them three-fourths full to allow for expansion. Put each bottle in a small ziplock plastic bag for further protection.

Passport Information

Make sure your passport is up-to-date (and isn't scheduled to expire until at least six months after the trip). Visas are required prior to departure for some countries in the Middle East. (Individuals with U.S. passports do not need to obtain a visa prior to their trip to Israel; a tourist visa will be issued to them at passport control on arrival.) Travel agencies will usually take care of obtaining required visas for individuals. Check with them if you have any questions. Keep your passport with you in a safe place at all times. Also, keep a photocopy of your passport in a separate location, possibly inside your suitcase. Remember, do not pack your passport inside your suitcase!

If you plan to obtain a passport for the first time, instructions for applying for your passport are found on pages 29–31. The key tip for first-time applicants is to apply early!

Photography

If your camera uses film, make sure you take plenty. (Film is expensive overseas.) Also, take an extra set of batteries for your camera. You may wish to invest in a lead-lined bag to hold your film to avoid any X-ray damage. You may be required to unload your camera for inspection when boarding planes, so the best policy is to make sure you have no film in your camera when you arrive at the airport. (For your convenience, at the end of this guide we have included a film list for recording each picture.)

A digital camera can be a wise investment for a trip far from home: It allows you to review your pictures immediately (and reshoot if necessary), and it also provides you with photos to look at during your flight home. But if you are taking a digital camera, be sure to bring sufficient memory cards or sticks to store pictures. Another alternative is to download your pictures to a portable storage device during the trip. Finally, make sure you bring the cable for recharging your camera's internal battery!

Use discretion in what you photograph—especially military personnel, secure areas (like airports and military bases), Muslim women with covered faces, or Orthodox Jewish men and women. If you are in doubt, ask first!

Physical Exercise

You will be doing a great deal of walking on your trip. It is strongly recommended that you do some walking now—in the shoes you're taking on the tour—to condition yourself. If you're buying new shoes for the trip, plan to wear them weeks before departure so they are "broken in" and you are comfortable walking in them.

Shopping

The English language is spoken sufficiently everywhere, so no language problem need arise. Part of the fun of shopping is the Middle Eastern culture of "bargaining" for an item. When bargaining with merchants, don't appear too anxious to purchase an item, and never accept the first price as the actual price. In many cases the item can be purchased for less than half of the "asking price." The truth of Proverbs 20:14 will come alive in the markets of the Middle East. "'Bad, bad,' says the buyer, but when he goes his way, then he boasts" (NASB).

Keep a written record of all your purchases, as this will make the filing of your customs report easier when you return home. Be careful about exposing much money at any one time when you are shopping.

Telephone

Calls to the United States can be placed through the switchboard at all hotels. However, most hotels add a hefty service charge for this service. Consider purchasing a prepaid calling card available at most discount stores here in the U.S. Check with the company issuing the card to obtain the appropriate access number for calling to the United States from the different countries to which you are traveling—and to make sure the card can be used in that country.

U.S. cellular phones can be used overseas only if they are quad-band GSM phones. If you have any questions, check with your provider to find out if your cell phone will work overseas. It is often more cost-effective simply to rent a cell phone with prepaid minutes while traveling overseas. (In most cases incoming calls to these phones are free.) Check with your travel agent to see if this is a possibility.

Traveling as Part of a Group

Sometimes photographers will take pictures of you or your group. You are not obligated to buy any. Expect some inconveniences such as schedule changes. Things do not always run as smoothly as they do in the United States. Have a good Christian attitude about it all.

Be careful about sharing your faith. This is an especially sensitive situation in the Middle East. Let your life and conduct count. Consider the believers there whose situation you might make more difficult by arousing anger or by giving a poor testimony. Pray for the tour. Live with others as Christians should; plan to cooperate and stay on schedule with the group. The guide and tour host are concerned for the welfare of the entire group, and they count on your cooperation to make it an enjoyable time for all.

Weather

The climate of Israel, Greece, Jordan, and the southern part of Turkey is often described as Mediterranean. This type of climate is known for its hot, dry summers and cold, rainy winters. Other parts of Turkey have a climate that is more akin to Europe. Egypt is a desert climate with very little rainfall.

Israel

Winter weather in Israel is very changeable, and November through March is the rainy season. While you should have some beautiful days, expect to see rain, especially in the hill country. The average temperature can vary greatly depending on where you are in Israel. Expect cool days and cold nights in Jerusalem. Following are the average high/low temperatures for various places in Israel in the winter.

	Nov.	Dec.	Jan.	Feb.	March
Jerusalem	67/54	56/47	53/43	57/44	61/47
Tel Aviv	76/54	66/47	65/49	66/48	69/51
Sea of Galilee	78/59	68/53	65/48	67/49	72/51
Dead Sea	83/61	74/51	70/49	73/51	79/56

Spring and summer weather is very stable and pleasant. April and May can still bring occasional rain, but little or no rain will fall from June through October. The average summer temperature can still vary greatly. Expect warm days and cool nights in Jerusalem. The following are the average high/low temperatures for various places in Israel in the summer.

	April	May	June	July	August
Jerusalem	69/53	77/60	81/63	84/66	86/66
Tel Aviv	72/54	77/63	83/67	86/70	86/72
Sea of Galilee	80/56	89/62	95/68	98/73	99/75
Dead Sea	87/63	95/69	99/75	103/77	104/79

Egypt

Winter weather in Egypt is mild and predictable, with warm days and cool nights. While October through March is the rainy season, Egypt is very dry except for along the Mediterranean coast. Cairo's annual average rainfall is about 2 inches, and that total decreases to .04 inches in Aswan. It is not unusual for some parts of Egypt to report no rainfall in a year.

Early spring weather in Egypt is generally comfortable. However, this is the time of year when there can be large fluctuations in temperature, particularly when the *khamsin* wind prevails. The *khamsin* is a very hot, dry wind that blows from the south and southeast, raising the temperature by up to twenty degrees in a matter of hours. These rapid rises in temperature don't last long, but they are often followed by dust/sand storms accompanying a cold front.

Following are the average high/low temperatures for various places in Egypt throughout the winter and early spring.

	Nov.	Dec.	Jan.	Feb.	March
Aswan	86/58	79/50	75/46	79/49	86/54
Cairo	75/54	69/51	66/47	69/48	75/52
Luxor	78/59	68/53	74/42	78/44	84/51
Red Sea	83/61	74/51	75/64	77/64	79/68

Late spring and summer weather in Egypt is stable and hot.

April can still see warm days and cool nights, but by May the days are becoming extremely hot. The temperature is made more bearable by very low levels of humidity, but this raises the concern of rapid dehydration. Proper hydration is essential in the summer months; drink plenty of water.

Following are the average high/low temperatures for various places in Egypt in the late spring and summer.

	April	May	June	July	August
Aswan	97/63	101/71	108/76	108/76	108/84
Cairo	83/56	90/63	95/68	96/71	95/71
Luxor	95/60	103/69	107/72	108/76	107/76
Red Sea	88/77	95/79	99/82	107/82	108/84

Greece

Winter weather in Greece is very changeable, and November through March is the rainy season. While you should have some beautiful days, expect to see periods of rain. The average temperature can vary greatly depending on where you are in Greece. Following are the average high/low temperatures for various places in Greece throughout the winter and early spring.

	Nov.	Dec.	Jan.	Feb.	March
Athens	64/53	58/47	55/44	55/44	60/47
Iráklion, Crete	66/56	61/51	58/48	58/48	61/50
Thessaloníki	58/44	51/37	48/34	51/36	57/41

Spring and summer weather is stable and pleasant. April and May can still see occasional rain, but little or no rain will fall from June through October. The average summer temperature can still vary greatly. Expect warm days and pleasant nights.

Following are the average high/low temperatures for various places in Greece in the late spring and summer.

	April	May	June	July	August
Athens	66/52	74/60	83/67	88/72	88/72
Iráklion, Crete	67/54	73/59	80/66	83/72	82/71
Thessaloníki	65/46	75/54	84/62	88/66	87/65

Jordan

Winter weather in Jordan is very changeable, and November through March is the rainy season. While you should have some beautiful days, expect to see rain, especially in the hills near Amman. The average temperature can vary greatly depending on where you are in the country. Expect cool days and cold nights in the higher elevations. Following are the average high/low temperatures for various places in Jordan throughout the winter and early spring.

	Nov.	Dec.	Jan.	Feb.	March
Amman	70/50	59/43	54/39	55/39	61/43
Aqaba	75/54	69/51	68/50	71/53	78/58
Petra	78/61	68/53	65/50	69/54	75/59

Spring and summer weather is stable and pleasant. April and May can still see occasional rain, but little or no rain will fall from June through October. The average summer temperature can still vary greatly. Expect warm days and cool nights in Amman. Following are the average high/low temperatures for various places in Jordan in the late spring and summer.

	April	May	June	July	August
Amman	73/48	82/57	88/61	90/64	91/66
Aqaba	87/65	94/72	100/77	102/80	102/80
Petra	85/67	92/73	97/78	99/81	98/81

Turkey

Winter weather in Turkey is cool and wet. While several hours of sunshine can be expected each day, less than half the days in each month can be expected to be rain free. Cool days and cold nights are common in the higher elevations. Following are the average high/low temperatures for various places in Turkey throughout the winter and early spring.

	Nov.	Dec.	Jan.	Feb.	March
Istanbul	57/47	50/42	46/37	47/37	51/40
Kusadasi (Ephesus)	64/48	59/42	55/39	57/41	60/42
Denizli (Laodicea/Colossae)	62/42	51/37	50/33	51/35	59/39

Spring and summer weather is very stable and pleasant, although it can rain even during the summer. Expect warm days with abundant sunshine. Following are the average high/low temperatures for various places in Turkey in the late spring and summer.

	April	May	June	July	August
Istanbul	60/47	69/54	78/62	82/66	82/67
Kusadasi (Ephesus)	66/48	75/53	82/60	86/64	86/64
Denizli (Laodicea/Colossae)	68/46	77/53	86/60	91/66	91/64

PACKING LIST

The following list is intended to help you pack more efficiently. If you have any special needs, be sure to add those items to your list. Items with an asterisk (*) may be optional.

Clothing

- blouses, shirts, socks, underwear (take a limited supply—use wash-and-wear)
- shorts, slacks, jeans, skirts (take a limited supply)
- personal modesty kit (for entering "holy places" and conservative communities)
- heavy sweater or jacket
- swimsuit
- walking shoes (plenty of walking! Good shoes are very important!)
- flip-flops or old sneakers (for the beach)

- sunglasses
- hat

Toiletries / Medications

- shampoo
- toothbrush and paste, dental floss
- deodorant
- personal soap (hotel will furnish small bars)*
- comb and hairbrush
- nail clippers, file
- shaving equipment
- eyedrops or contact lens solutions and cleaners*
- other personal hygiene products
- athlete's foot treatment, Band-Aids
- diarrhea medicine (just in case!)
- cold remedy or decongestant tablets
- sleeping pills
- motion sickness pills
- aspirin or other nonprescription medications
- copies of any prescriptions (in case you need them filled)
- sunscreen/lotion, sunburn medication/ointment
- package of towelettes*
- earplugs

Miscellaneous

- travel alarm
- plastic bags (for wet washcloth, laundry, etc.)
- pen, notebook, and small Bible (Old and New Testament)
- small sewing kit

- adapter or converter for all electrical appliances
- tiny flashlight
- handkerchiefs or tissues
- laundry detergent (small supply)*
- washcloth*
- camera, film, extra batteries, extra memory stick for digital camera
- extra pair of eyeglasses (or prescription)
- electrical appliances (hair dryer, razor, travel iron)*
- cassette recorder*
- small umbrella or rain hat (November–April)
- boxed snacks (individually packed, travel size)*

Items to Pack in Hand Luggage

- airline tickets
- passport
- one-day change of clothes
- essential toiletries
- neck pillow and sleeping mask (for sleeping on airplane)
- good book(s) (to read on the flight over and back)

REQUIREMENTS FOR OBTAINING A U.S. PASSPORT

If you have never traveled abroad, it is wise to apply for a passport early, as it can take up to six weeks to process a passport request. The government can expedite a passport application, but they charge a significant premium for that service. Travelers who plan ahead can avoid the stress—and additional charge—of a last-minute application. Consider applying for your passport at least three months prior to your scheduled date of departure.

If you currently have a valid passport that is scheduled to expire within six months of your trip, you should also renew your passport before you go. Some countries are reluctant to admit travelers whose passports will expire within six months of entry. Renewing your passport now will help avoid potential complications while on the trip. (See point 3a for how to renew a passport.)

1. Obtain a passport application from your district or county clerk's office (usually at the county courthouse), the post office, or your local travel agency. This form can also be downloaded from the U.S. Department of State Web site, **http://www.travel.state.gov/passport**. The Web site includes a very helpful "Frequently Asked Questions" section with current information on fees and policies. It is wise to visit this site before applying for a new passport.

2. Fill out the application and take it back to the district clerk with the following additional items. (Call your local office to see if you need to arrange an appointment time to appear with your application. The phone numbers for the various offices can be found at the Department of State Web site listed above.)

a. A certified birth certificate with state, city, or county seal. Hospital birth certificates or "notification of birth" certificates are not acceptable. You must present a certified birth certificate.

b. Two identical, recently made 2 x 2 inch photos with image size between 1 and 1 3/8 inches from bottom of chin to top of hair with plain white background. Photos must be clear, front view, full face, taken in normal street attire (no hats or dark glasses). These photos can be obtained at most camera shops and photography studios—and at many office supply stores and copy centers—with no wait and at a reasonable price.

c. A valid driver's license, a military ID, or a state-issued picture ID.

d. A check or money order for the cost of the passport payable to "U.S. Department of State." (They will not accept cash for this amount.) Currently this totals $67, which includes a $12 security surcharge. In addition, you must bring $30 for the execution fee. (Some offices may not accept a personal check for this portion; to find out, call the office you'll be going to.)

e. Your Social Security number.

f. Applicants ages fourteen through seventeen must appear in person at the district clerk's office. Application for minors under the age of fourteen must be done in person by the minor and requires both parents or the legal guardian to give consent and at least one parent or guardian appear with the child.

g. Certified proof of name change (required only if your name is different than that appearing on your birth certificate), such as a marriage license.

3. The above fee information applies to all new passport applications for individuals sixteen years of age and older. Following are some exceptions for those renewing their passport and for those under age sixteen.

a. To renew your passport you only need to obtain an application for passport renewal from the district clerk, the post office, your local travel agency, or online (see previous page for Web address). You can mail the application (along with your old or expired passport) directly to the regional passport office listed on the form with, of course, a check for $67. No execution fee is required when your old passport is included with the mailed application.

b. The fee to "U.S. Department of State" for applicants fifteen years of age or younger is only $40, plus the security surcharge of $12. Thus the total (before the required $30 execution fee) is $52.

4. Please keep your receipt until your passport and submitted documents have been returned to you.

5. If you already have a valid passport but have changed your name, you must get your passport changed. This is done without charge. Forms to update your passport can be obtained from the district clerk, the post office, your local travel agency, or online (see previous page for Web address).

HOW TO OVERCOME JET LAG

Rapid travel through multiple time zones can take its toll on the traveler's physical and mental well-being. "Jet lag" is the phrase used to describe the condition when an individual's internal body clock is out of sync with the actual time in the region to which he or she has traveled. The clock on the wall says that it is the middle of the night, but the traveler's body awakens and refuses to go back to sleep. Jet lag can result in lethargy, sleeplessness, constipation or diarrhea, and illness. At the very least it can make a person feel "out of sorts" for the first two or three days of the trip.

Several simple techniques have been developed to help an individual overcome the symptoms of jet lag and adjust his or her internal body clock to the new time zone as rapidly as possible. These principles are used by government employees who travel around the world and who must operate at peak efficiency the minute they arrive. The principles are explained fully in the book *Overcoming Jet Lag* (Berkley Publishing), by Charles F. Ehret and Lynne Waller Scanlon. The following information is loosely adapted from the book and applied specifically to flights to the Middle East. If you follow these principles, you will find that your body will adjust very rapidly to the change in time zones.

The time difference between the eastern United States and the Middle East is seven hours. That is, when it is noon in New York City, it is 7:00 p.m. in Amman, Istanbul, and Jerusalem. Similarly, when you bed down at 10 p.m. in Athens or Cairo, it's only three in the afternoon back home in New York City. The following instructions will help you overcome jet lag while touring the Middle East. It is sometimes difficult to follow these principles exactly, but the more you are able to follow them, the easier you will find it to adjust your internal body clock.

The Day of the Flight

- Get out of bed earlier than usual.
- Eat a high-protein breakfast and lunch, and try to eat a high-carbohydrate supper during the flight.
- Drink a lot of water or decaffeinated beverages to compensate for the dehydration that is common on long flights.

- Shortly after the evening meal on your transatlantic flight, set your wristwatch ahead to your destination time.
- Since it is now early morning destination time, try to rest or sleep as soon as possible. Pull down your window shade, put on a sleeping mask, or take a sleeping aid—but go to sleep!

Breakfast, Destination Time

- Do not oversleep. Walk around to activate your body and brain.
- Drink one to two cups of black coffee, strong tea, or caffeinated soft drinks between 6:00 and 8:00 a.m. destination time or when breakfast is served on the airplane.
- Keep active. Do not nap! Go to bed by 10:00 p.m. destination time. Even though you feel tired, consider taking a sleeping aid to make sure you sleep through the night.
- If you wake up in the middle of the night, try to go back to sleep.

First Touring Day

Your body should be almost adjusted to the change in time zones. Eat well, keep active, don't allow yourself to nap, and enjoy your time on tour. Take a sleeping aid for the last time that night.

HELPFUL WEB SITES

The Internet is an excellent source of information to help someone prepare for a trip to the Middle East. Unfortunately, many Web sites do not remain accessible for a long period of time. The following links were chosen because of their helpfulness and because of their long-term stability.

General Sites to Assist in Travel to the Middle East

- Currency Converter (**http://www.oanda.com/convert/classic** use http on each Internet address on the World Wide Web.)
- Centers for Control and Prevention (**www.cdc.gov/travel**)
- Passport Information (**www.travel.state.gov/passport**)

- Photographs of Israel, Jordan, Egypt, Turkey, and Greece (**www.bibleplaces.com**)
- U.S. State Department Travel Warnings and Consular Information Sheets (**www.travel.state.gov/travel**)

Israel

- *Haaretz* Newspaper (**www.haaretzdaily.com**)
- Israel Ministry of Tourism (**www.goisrael.com**)
- Israel Museum (**www.imj.org.il/index.asp?news2=1**)
- *Jerusalem Post* Newspaper (**www.jpost.com**)
- Jewish Virtual Library (**www.jewishvirtuallibrary.org**)

Egypt

- Egyptian Museum (**www.egyptianmuseum.gov.eg**)
- Egyptian Tourist Authority (**www.egypttourism.org**)
- Virtual Egyptian Museum (**www.virtual-egyptian-museum.org**)

Greece

- Athens Survival Guide (**www.athensguide.com**)
- Tourism in Greece (**www.greek-tourism.gr** and **www.greeka.com/greece/greece-tourism.htm**)

Jordan

- Jordan Tourism Board (**www.see-jordan.com**)

Turkey

- Turkey Ministry of Culture and Tourism (**www.tourismturkey.org** and **www.kultur.gov.tr/EN**)

A Four-Week Schedule of Bible Reading and Prayer —To Prepare for Israel

	Bible Readings	Items for Prayer
Week #1:	*Focus on the Land*	*Pray for the Group*
Day 1	Deuteronomy 8:6–20	Safety of the group
Day 2	Deuteronomy 11:8–21	Physical health and strength of the group
Day 3	Psalm 42	Unity and harmony of the group
Day 4	Psalm 121	Spirit of excitement among the group
Day 5	Proverbs 24:30–34	Joyful attitude among the group
Day 6	Isaiah 40:1–11	Smooth travel arrangements for the group
Day 7	Luke 8:4–15	The forging of new friendships within the group
Week #2:	*Focus on Galilee*	*Pray for Those Who Assist the Tour*
Day 1	Isaiah 9:1–7	The guides
Day 2	Luke 4:14–30	The bus drivers
Day 3	Matthew 4:18–5:12	The tour host or pastor

Day 4	John 2:1–11	The travel agent and land operator
Day 5	Matthew 8:5–17	The airline pilots and flight attendants
Day 6	Mark 5:35–43	The airport baggage handlers
Day 7	Matthew 16:13–28	The hotel staff
Week #3:	*Focus on the Hill Country*	*Pray for Yourself*
Day 1	Joshua 10:1–15	Ability to retain information
Day 2	Joshua 24:1–15	Spiritual discernment
Day 3	1 Samuel 17:1–50	Adaptability and flexibility
Day 4	1 Kings 18:16–46	A spirit of anticipation
Day 5	2 Kings 17:5–23	Physical strength and stamina
Day 6	Nehemiah 4:1–15	Personal safety
Day 7	John 4:1–42	A Christlike attitude
Week #4:	*Focus on Jerusalem*	*Pray for the Physical Arrangements*
Day 1	Psalm 122	Good weather
Day 2	Psalm 125	Comfort on the airline flights
Day 3	Matthew 21:1–17	Safe road conditions
Day 4	Mark 14:12–52	Quiet, comfortable hotels
Day 5	Luke 24	Reliable buses
Day 6	Acts 2	Careful handling of all luggage
Day 7	Zechariah 14:1–9	Smooth travel connections

—To Prepare for Egypt and Jordan

	Bible Readings	Items for Prayer
Week #1:	*Focus on Egypt*	*Pray for the Group*
Day 1	Genesis 12:10–20; 16:1	Safety of the group
Day 2	Hebrews 11:23–29	Physical health and strength of the group
Day 3	Exodus 1:8–14	Unity and harmony of the group
Day 4	Exodus 2:1–10	Spirit of excitement among the group
Day 5	Exodus 5:1–21	Joyful attitude among the group
Day 6	Exodus 12:1–42	Smooth travel arrangements for the group
Day 7	Exodus 13:17–14:31	The forging of new friendships within the group
Week #2:	*Focus on the Wilderness*	*Pray for Those Who Assist the Tour*
Day 1	Exodus 3:1–12	The guides
Day 2	Exodus 15:22–27	The bus drivers
Day 3	Exodus 17	The tour leaders

Day 4	Exodus 32	The travel agent and land operator
Day 5	Numbers 13:17–14:38	The airline pilots and flight attendants
Day 6	Numbers 20:1–13	The airport baggage handlers
Day 7	Psalm 90	The hotel staff
Week #3:	*Focus on Transjordan*	*Pray for Yourself*
Day 1	Numbers 21:4–13	Ability to retain information
Day 2	Numbers 21:21–26	Spiritual discernment
Day 3	Numbers 32:1–22	Adaptability and flexibility
Day 4	Deuteronomy 2:1–23	A spirit of anticipation
Day 5	Deuteronomy 2:24–37	Physical strength and stamina
Day 6	Psalm 78:9–39	Personal safety
Day 7	Micah 6:3–5	A Christlike attitude
Week #4:	*Focus on the Final Camp*	*Pray for the Physical Arrangements*
Day 1	Numbers 22:1–6, 21–35	Good weather
Day 2	Numbers 23:1–26	Comfort on the airline flights
Day 3	Numbers 23:27–24:25	Safe road conditions
Day 4	Numbers 25	Quiet, comfortable hotels
Day 5	Deuteronomy 34	Reliable buses
Day 6	Joshua 2	Careful handling of all luggage
Day 7	Joshua 3	Smooth travel connections

—To Prepare for Greece and Turkey

	Bible Readings	Items for Prayer
Week #1:	*Focus on Paul in Turkey*	*Pray for the Group*
Day 1	Acts 16:1–10	Safety of the group
Day 2	Acts 18:24–28	Physical health and strength of the group
Day 3	Acts 19:1–22	Unity and harmony of the group
Day 4	Acts 19:23–41	Spirit of excitement among the group
Day 5	Acts 20:17–38	Joyful attitude among the group
Day 6	Book of Ephesians	Smooth travel arrangements for the group
Day 7	Book of Colossians	The forging of new friendships within the group
Week #2:	*Focus on Paul in Greece*	*Pray for Those Who Assist the Tour*
Day 1	Acts 16:11–40	The guides
Day 2	Acts 17:1–15	The bus drivers
Day 3	Acts 17:16–34	The tour leaders

Day 4	Acts 18:1–17	The travel agent and land operator
Day 5	Book of 1 Thessalonians	The airline pilots and flight attendants
Day 6	Book of 1 Corinthians	The airport baggage handlers
Day 7	Book of Philippians	The hotel staff
Week #3:	*Focus on the Aegean*	*Pray for Yourself*
Day 1	Acts 20:13–16; 21:1–4	Ability to retain information
Day 2	Acts 27:1–13	Spiritual discernment
Day 3	Acts 27:14–44	Adaptability and flexibility
Day 4	Titus 1	A spirit of anticipation
Day 5	Titus 2	Physical strength and stamina
Day 6	Titus 3	Personal safety
Day 7	Revelation 1	A Christlike attitude
Week #4:	*Focus on Revelation*	*Pray for the Physical Arrangements*
Day 1	Revelation 2:1–7	Good weather
Day 2	Revelation 2:8–11	Comfort on the airline flights
Day 3	Revelation 2:12–17	Safe road conditions
Day 4	Revelation 2:18–29	Quiet, comfortable hotels
Day 5	Revelation 3:1–6	Reliable buses
Day 6	Revelation 3:7–13	Careful handling of all luggage
Day 7	Revelation 3:14–22	Smooth travel connections

A Four-Week Bible Series to Prepare a Group Spiritually for a Trip to Israel

Week #1 TRUST AND OBEY
Deuteronomy 11:1–32
God's Testing Ground of Faith

I. God's Expectations (11:1–12)

A. God expects us to love and obey Him because of what He has done for us in the past (11:1–7).

NOTE: *God rehearses Israel's history from their bondage in Egypt, through their deliverance at the Red Sea . . . to their judgment in the wilderness.*

B. God expects us to love and obey Him because of His promises to us for the future (11:8–12).

NOTE: *God describes the Promised Land to a nation that has not yet experienced it.*

1. It's a land of promised blessing (v. 9).

2. It's a land unlike anything experienced before (v. 10).

3. It's a land under God's care (vv. 11–12).

II. God's Response (11:13–21)

A. God will bless those who trust and obey Him (11:13–15).
1. God will provide the needed rain (vv. 13–14a).

NOTE: *Israel's rainy season extends from late November to early March, but in a good year the rains begin in October and extend into April. The "early rain and the latter rain" are these extensions and signal abundant rainfall and a good harvest.*

2. God will provide the needed food (for the people and their animals; vv. 14b–15).

NOTE: *The "grain" refers to wheat and barley, Israel's main food source. The "wine" comes from the vineyards, and the "oil" from the olive tree. These are four of the seven main species of the land that God promised Israel (see Deut. 8:7–8).*

B. God will judge those who turn from Him (11:16–21).

1. God's warning against turning from Him (vv. 16–17)

2. God's remedy for turning from Him (vv. 18–21)

a. Know His Word (v. 18).

NOTE: *Orthodox Jews today take this literally and bind phylacteries on their arms and foreheads when praying.*

b. Teach His Word (v. 19).

c. Exalt His Word in the home and in the city (vv. 20–21).

NOTE: *Orthodox Jews today take this literally and place mezuzahs (a box containing a portion of God's Word) on the door frames of their homes and businesses and on the gates of the city of Jerusalem.*

III. **God's Reminder** (11:22–32)

A. God reminded the people of His promises before they entered the land (11:22–25).

1. Obedience brings victory over opposition (vv. 22–23).

2. Obedience brings victory over limitations (v. 24).

3. Obedience brings victory over obstacles (v. 25).

B. God commanded the people to remember His promises after they entered the land (11:26–32).

NOTE: *Israel fulfilled this command in Joshua 8:30–35. Mount Ebal and Mount Gerizim today stand guard over the Arab city of Nablus.*

Conclusion

The land of Israel was God's "testing ground of faith." God expected His children to move ahead by faith and take the land He had promised them. But their walk of faith was not to end once the land had been conquered. God wants His followers to live out His command to "trust and obey."

NOTE: *Conclude with the hymn "Trust and Obey."*

Week #2 IT IS WELL WITH MY SOUL
Isaiah 40:1–31
Comfort in Times of Discouragement

I. **The Announcement of Comfort** (40:1–5)

A. The announcement from God in heaven (40:1–2)

NOTE: *The three promises of God foreshadow the three main themes of Isaiah 40–66.*

1. "Her warfare is accomplished" looks to Israel's deliverance from Babylon (Isaiah 40–48).

2. "Her iniquity is pardoned" looks to Israel's redemption from sin (Isaiah 49–57).

3. "She has received . . . double" looks to Israel's double portion of blessing in the future (Isaiah 58–66) [For this use of "double" see Isa. 61:7.].

B. The announcement from "a voice in the wilderness" (40:3–5)

NOTE: *The "wilderness" being described is the Judean Wilderness that lies between Jerusalem and Jericho and along the western edge of the Dead Sea. Verse 4 is a perfect picture of this land and offers hope by showing that God can "change the unchangeable."*

1. The call to preparation (v. 3)

2. The removal of all obstacles (v. 4)

3. The appearance of God's glory (v. 5)

II. The Reasons for Comfort (40:6–26)

A. The certainty of God's Word (40:6–8)

1. People are temporal (vv. 6–8a).

NOTE: *Isaiah describes the grass and flowers that grow in the Judean Wilderness during the winter rainy season. Once the rains end and the hot east wind blows in from the Arabian Desert, the grass and flowers wither and die.*

2. God's Word stands forever (v. 8b).

NOTE: *People, problems, and circumstances come and go just like the wildflowers in the Judean Wilderness. But we can find hope in God's Word of promise, which will never fail.*

B. The surety of God's character (40:9–26)

1. God's power and love are constant (vv. 9–11).

NOTE: *Isaiah challenges the people to look closely at the character of the God offering them comfort and deliverance.*

a. God has the might of a conquering hero (v. 10).

b. God has the compassion of a tender shepherd (v. 11).

2. God's strength is mightier than any opposition (vv. 12–26).

NOTE: *Isaiah asks, and answers, a series of questions to show that God is superior to any possible opposition we might face. Our God is bigger than our problems!*

a. God is superior to nations (vv. 12–17).

(1) The questions (vv. 12–14)

(2) The application to God (vv. 15–17)

b. God is superior to idols (vv. 18–20).

(1) The questions (v. 18)

(2) The application to God (vv. 19–20)

c. God is superior to human leaders (vv. 21–24).

(1) The questions (v. 21)

(2) The application to God (vv. 22–24)

d. God is superior to all cosmic forces (vv. 25–26).

(1) The questions (v. 25)

(2) The application to God (v. 26)

III. The Requirements for Receiving Comfort (40:27–31)

A. Remember God's goodness (40:27–28).

1. The complaint: God doesn't know or care for me (v. 27).

2. The solution: Realize God's awesome character and power (v. 28).

a. God made all.

b. God sustains all.

c. God understands all.

B. Wait on God to solve your problems (40:29–31).

1. Human strength will fail (vv. 29–30).

2. Those who depend on God's strength will succeed (v. 31).

Conclusion

The Judean Wilderness served as an object lesson to the nation of Israel. It stood as an obstacle between Jerusalem and Jericho—harsh, foreboding, and unchangeable. It symbolized their problems that often seemed overwhelming, unsolvable, and utterly discouraging. God's reminder in times of trouble is to focus on Him, not on our problems. He is mightier than our problems and stronger than our opposition. And He desires to bear us up on wings of eagles. The God who can change the craggy wilderness into a smooth plain is the God who can cause us to say—even as we face our trials—"It is well with my soul!"

NOTE: *Conclude with the hymn "It Is Well with My Soul."*

Week #3 A GREAT PROPHET IN OUR MIDST!
2 Kings 4:8–37; Luke 7:11–17
The Ministries of Elisha and Jesus

I. Elisha's Ministry in Shunem (2 Kings 4:8–37)

A. The birth of a child (4:8–17)

NOTE: *The village of Shunem rests on the southern slopes of the Hill of Moreh. Prior to the time of Elisha, this city had known terror . . . and honor. The Philistines captured the village and used it as their base when they gathered to fight against Saul and the Israelites (1 Sam. 28:4). Later a woman from Shunem named Abishag was chosen to take care of King David in his old age (1 Kings 1:3–4).*

1. The woman's kindness to Elisha (vv. 8–10)

2. Elisha's kindness to the woman (vv. 11–17)

NOTE: *In the Old Testament barrenness was a sign of cursing. The woman displayed faith in recognizing Elisha as a prophet, and she displayed compassion in providing for his needs. God blessed her with fruitfulness for her kindness.*

B. The "second birth" of the child (4:18–37)

NOTE: *After the miraculous birth of the child, one expects the family to live "happily ever after." The sudden death of the child was a severe test of the woman's faith, but her quick, decisive response revealed her depth of trust.*

1. The child's death (vv. 18–21)

NOTE: *The child went out to his father who was "with the reapers." This would place the event in the spring during wheat or barley harvest. The sun can become brutally hot in the late morning, and the cooling breeze from the Mediterranean doesn't usually arrive until the early afternoon. The child may have been overcome by the intense morning sun because he died at noon (v. 20).*

2. The woman's journey to Elisha (vv. 22–30)

NOTE: *The woman rode across the Jezreel Valley from Shunem to Mount Carmel in the heat of the day to summon Elisha.*

3. Elisha's miracle of restoring the boy to life (vv. 32–37)

NOTE: *After raising the son to life, Elisha gave the son back to the mother. "Then she took her son and went out" (v. 37).*

The scene now shifts forward in time nine hundred years to another small town on the Hill of Moreh.

II. Jesus' Ministry in Nain (Luke 7:11–17)

A. Jesus' arrival in the village (7:11–13)

NOTE: *The village of Nain rests on the northern slopes of the Hill of Moreh, approximately two miles from Shunem. The parallels to Elisha's miracle in the area are obvious . . . and intentional.*

1. The event takes place on the slopes of the Hill of Moreh.

2. The dead child is an only son.

3. The account focuses on the response of the mother.

4. Each account focuses on a man of God recognized as a prophet.

B. Jesus' raising of the widow's son (7:14–15)

1. Jesus restored the boy to life (v. 14).

2. Jesus gave the child back to his mother (v. 15).

NOTE: *Jesus' actions parallel those of Elisha. Elisha summoned the Shunammite woman and commanded her to "Take your son." Jesus gave the boy "back to his mother."*

C. The crowd's response to the miracle (7:16–17)

NOTE: *The crowd understood the significance of Jesus' miracle when they shouted, "A great prophet has appeared among us." No doubt they saw the connection between Jesus' miracle and the one performed by Elisha on the same mountain nearly nine hundred years earlier.*

Conclusion

Much of Jesus' ministry focused on visibly reminding the people of Israel that the God who had delivered them in the past was now at work in their midst. The miracles validated His claims to be God's Son, Israel's Messiah, and "the Prophet" promised by Moses. This particular story gives us a glimpse into God's compassion for those who are hurting. Just as Jesus' "heart went out to her" in her time of grief, so today Peter admonishes us to "cast all your anxiety on him because he cares for you" (1 Pet. 5:7).

NOTE: *Conclude with the hymn "Day by Day."*

Week #4 LEAD ME TO CALVARY
Matthew 26:57–28:10
The Events of the Crucifixion

I. The Cross (26:57–27:56)

A. The trials (26:57–27:26)

1. The trial before the Sanhedrin (26:57–75)

NOTE: *Peter denied Jesus during the time Jesus was appearing before the Jewish leaders in the high priest's house. Peter had followed at a distance, but when confronted he denied his Lord.*

2. The trial before Pilate (27:11–26)

NOTE: *Though the exact location is uncertain, tradition says that Jesus appeared before Pilate in the Fortress of Antonia that looked over the northwestern edge of the temple. From here Jesus began His walk to "The Place of the Skull."*

B. The torture (27:27–31)

NOTE: *The Romans flogged Jesus (v. 26), a lashing so severe that prisoners sometimes died from this punishment before being crucified. Jesus was then stripped, mocked, spat on, and beaten on the head with a staff. All this was "preparation" for the actual crucifixion.*

C. The crucifixion (27:32–56)

1. Jesus' journey to Golgotha (vv. 32–44)

NOTE: *Jesus likely carried a beam of the cross until, weakened by the flogging, He collapsed. The Romans forced a Jewish passerby to carry the beam the remainder of the way. From the cross Jesus could look out at soldiers gambling for His clothes, religious leaders mocking His death, and thieves sharing His dreaded fate.*

2. Jesus' death on the cross (vv. 45–56)

NOTE: *Crucifixion was a lengthy, torturous death. And yet, after paying for humanity's sin, Jesus "gave up his spirit." He did not die from the crucifixion. As He had said earlier, "I lay down my life—only to take it up again. No one takes it from me, but I lay it down of my own accord. I have authority to lay it down and authority to take it up again" (John 10:17–18).*

II. The Grave (27:57–66)

A. The burial at the tomb (27:57–61)

1. Joseph of Arimathea boldly requested the body of Jesus (vv. 57–58).

2. Joseph placed Jesus' body in his own new tomb (vv. 59–61).

NOTE: *In a "coincidence" prepared by God, Joseph's new tomb had been dug in the same area where Jesus was crucified. According to John's gospel, "At the place where Jesus was crucified, there was a garden, and in the garden a new tomb, in which no one had ever been laid" (John 19:41).*

B. The guarding of the tomb (27:62–66)

1. The request came from the religious leaders who remembered Jesus' words (vv. 62–64).

2. The order came from Pilate and was carried out by his soldiers (vv. 65–66).

NOTE: *The belief that the disciples stole Jesus' body contradicts this key fact: Jesus' tomb was sealed and under Roman guard. The frightened disciples would have been no match for experienced soldiers. In effect, God put the tomb under protective custody to validate the truth of the resurrection.*

III. The Empty Tomb (28:1–10)

A. The opening of the tomb (28:1–4)

B. The announcement to the women (28:5–10)

1. Jesus is risen.

2. The tomb is empty.

3. You will see Him.

Conclusion

God's "good news" for us is that Jesus died for our sins according to the Scriptures. His death was validated by His burial. He was raised on the third day according to the Scriptures. His resurrection was validated by His appearances to His disciples. Paul says this is the good news that he preached and by which we are saved (1 Cor. 15:1–8). During your coming visit to Jerusalem, you will walk the Via Dolorosa, stand at Calvary, and gaze into the empty tomb. And as you do, remember that Jesus suffered, died, and rose again . . . for you.

NOTE: *Conclude with the hymn "When I Survey the Wondrous Cross."*

P A R T   T W O

The Land of Israel

- The Twelve Tribes of Israel
- Map of the Twelve Tribes
- The History of Israel
- The Herods of the Bible
- Outline of Bible History

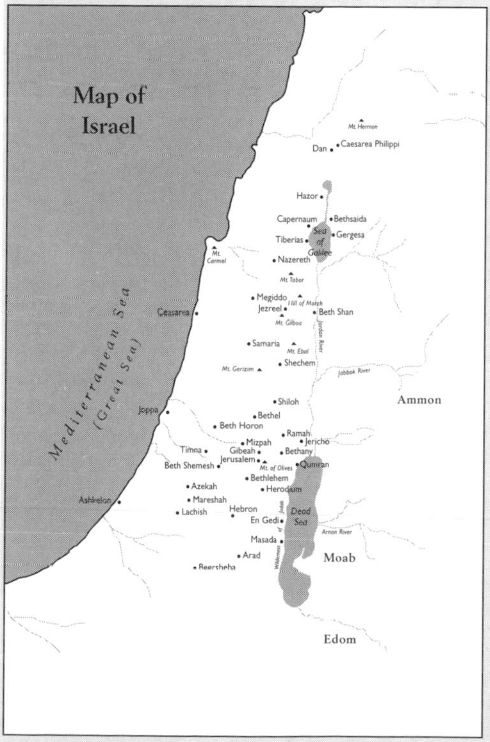

THE TWELVE TRIBES OF ISRAEL

The twelve tribes of Israel descended from the twelve sons of the patriarch Jacob, whom God later renamed Israel. The land assignments and relative importance of each tribe reflected the birth order, birth mother, and individual actions of each son. The allocation of land is shown on page 58.

Record of the Sons' Births

Genesis 29:31–30:24; 35:16–20

Key Historical Incidents in the Sons' Lives

Genesis 34:25–31
Simeon and Levi kill the men of Shechem.

Genesis 35:21–22
Reuben slept with his father's concubine.

Genesis 37:2–11
Joseph is hated by his brothers but is the favorite of his father.

Genesis 48:1–20
Jacob blesses Joseph's two children, Ephraim and Manasseh, and "adopts" them as his own.

Genesis 49:1–28
Jacob gives a prophetic blessing to each of his sons.

Tribal Allotments in the Land of Israel

Numbers 32:1–42
Allotment for Reuben, Gad, and one-half of Manasseh

Joshua 15:1–63
Allotment for Judah

Joshua 16:1–17:18
Allotment for Ephraim and one-half of Manasseh

Joshua 18:11–28
Allotment for Benjamin

Joshua 19:1–9
Allotment for Simeon

Joshua 19:10–16
Allotment for Zebulun

Joshua 19:17–23
Allotment for Issachar

Joshua 19:24–31
Allotment for Asher

Joshua 19:32–39
Allotment for Naphtali

Joshua 19:40–48
Allotment for Dan

Joshua 21:1–42
Allotment for Levi

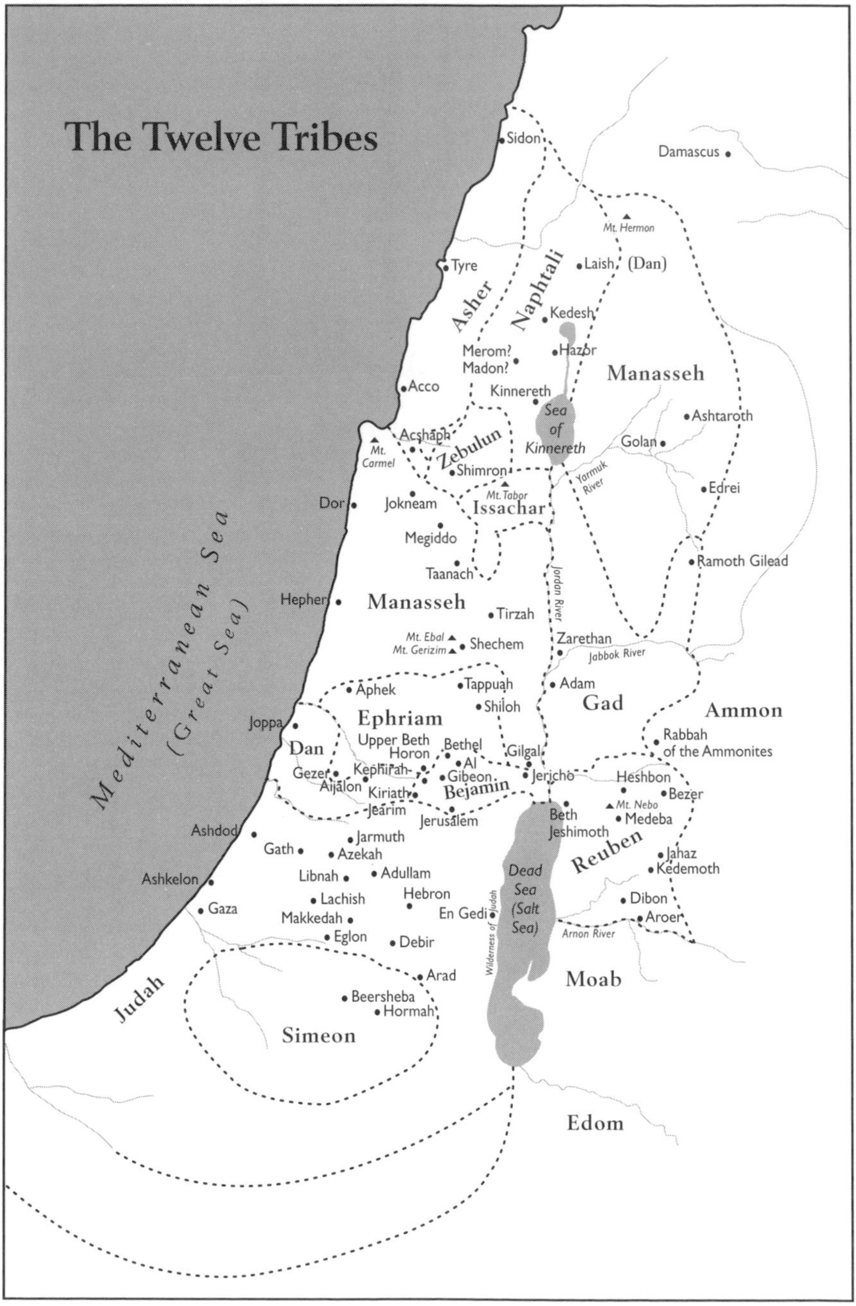
The Twelve Tribes
Sidon
Damascus
Mt. Hermon
Tyre
Laish
(Dan)
Asher
Naphtali
Kedesh
Merom?
Madon?
Hazor
Manasseh
Acco
Kinnereth
Sea of Kinnereth
Ashtaroth
Acshaph
Mt. Carmel
Zebulun
Golan
Shimron
Yarmuk River
Edrei
Mt. Tabor
Dor
Jokneam
Issachar
Megiddo
Ramoth Gilead
Taanach
Jordan River
Mediterranean Sea
(Great Sea)
Hepher
Manasseh
Tirzah
Mt. Ebal
Mt. Gerizim
Shechem
Zarethan
Jabbok River
Aphek
Tappuah
Adam
Shiloh
Gad
Ammon
Ephriam
Joppa
Dan
Upper Beth Horon
Bethel
Rabbah of the Ammonites
Gilgal
Ai
Gezer
Kephirah-
Gibeon
Jericho
Heshbon
Aijalon
Kiriath-Jearim
Bejamin
Bezer
Mt. Nebo
Beth Jeshimoth
Medeba
Jerusalem
Ashdod
Jarmuth
Gath
Azekah
Reuben
Jahaz
Kedemoth
Libnah
Adullam
Dead Sea (Salt Sea)
Ashkelon
Hebron
Lachish
Dibon
Gaza
Makkedah
En Gedi
Wilderness of Judah
Aroer
Arnon River
Eglon
Debir
Arad
Moab
Judah
Beersheba
Hormah
Simeon
Edom

The History of Israel

Date	Period	People and Events	World Events
	The Age of the Patriarchs	Abraham	
2000 BC		Isaac	
		Jacob	Hammurabi rules in Babylon
		Joseph	
	Israel grows into a nation in Egypt		
1500 BC			New Kingdom begins in Egypt
	Period of the Exodus and Conquest	Moses Joshua	
	Period of the Judges	Othniel Ehud Deborah and Barak Gideon Jephthah Samson Eli Samuel	Ruth and Boaz
1000 BC	The United Kingdom	Saul David Solomon	966 BC Solomon's Temple completed 931 BC The Kingdom is divided
	The Divided Kingdom	722 BC Israel falls to Assyria 586 BC Judah falls to Babylon	Assyrian Empire (c. 900–612 BC)
	Babylonian Captivity (586–539 BC)		Babylonian Empire (626–539 BC)
500 BC	Period of the Restoration	539 BC Jews return to the land 516 BC Temple rebuilt	Medo-Persian Empire (539–331 BC)
		Close of the Old Testament	

The Herods of the Bible

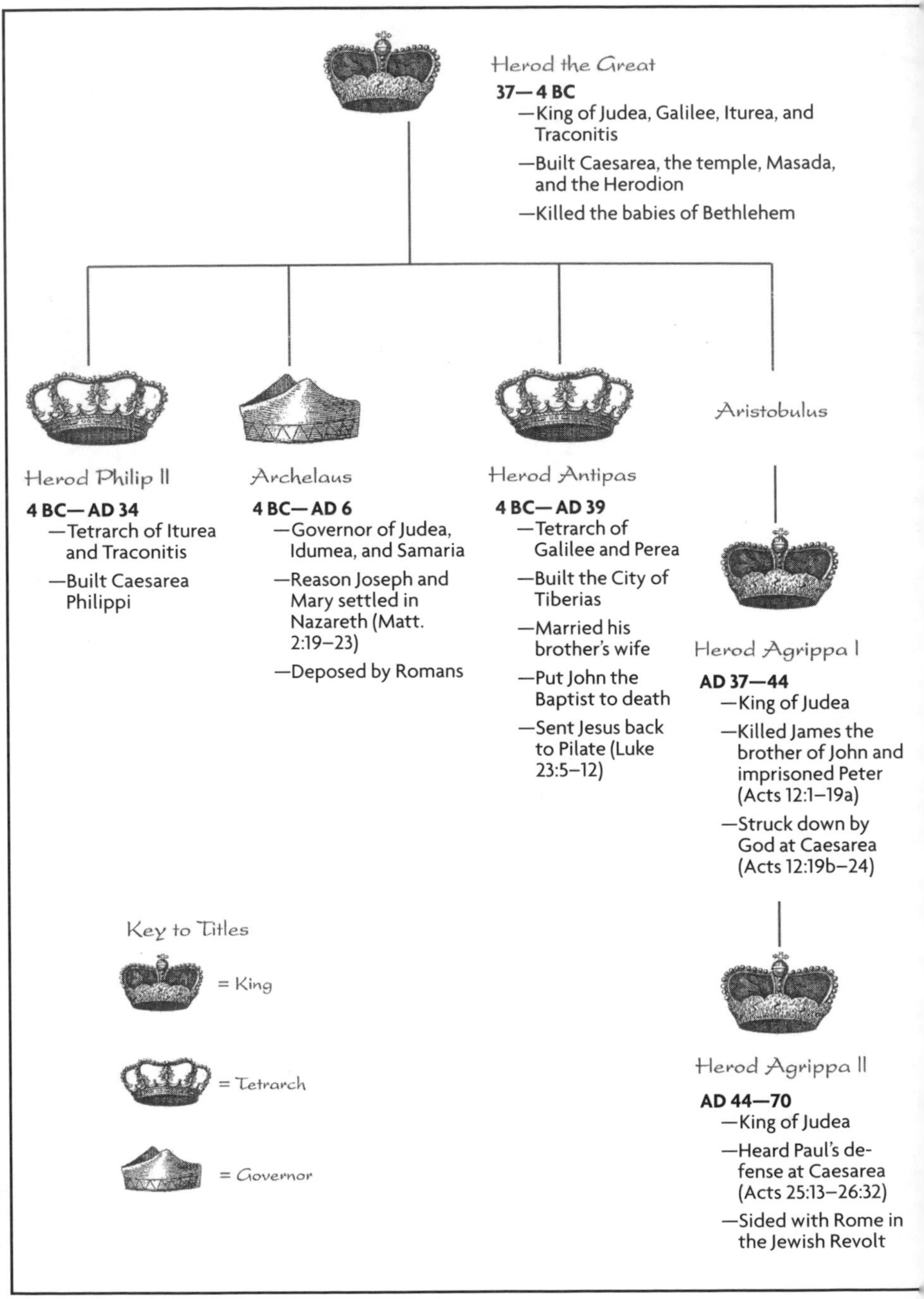
Herod the Great
37—4 BC
—King of Judea, Galilee, Iturea, and Traconitis
—Built Caesarea, the temple, Masada, and the Herodion
—Killed the babies of Bethlehem
Herod Philip II
4 BC—AD 34
—Tetrarch of Iturea and Traconitis
—Built Caesarea Philippi
Archelaus
4 BC—AD 6
—Governor of Judea, Idumea, and Samaria
—Reason Joseph and Mary settled in Nazareth (Matt. 2:19–23)
—Deposed by Romans
Herod Antipas
4 BC—AD 39
—Tetrarch of Galilee and Perea
—Built the City of Tiberias
—Married his brother's wife
—Put John the Baptist to death
—Sent Jesus back to Pilate (Luke 23:5–12)
Aristobulus
Herod Agrippa I
AD 37—44
—King of Judea
—Killed James the brother of John and imprisoned Peter (Acts 12:1–19a)
—Struck down by God at Caesarea (Acts 12:19b–24)
Herod Agrippa II
AD 44—70
—King of Judea
—Heard Paul's defense at Caesarea (Acts 25:13–26:32)
—Sided with Rome in the Jewish Revolt
Key to Titles
= King
= Tetrarch
= Governor

OUTLINE OF BIBLE HISTORY

The following chart contains a summary of the historical periods that relate to biblical events in the land of Israel. This chart will help you put the different locations you will visit in their proper historical setting.

BIBLICAL PERIOD	DATES	ARCHAEOLOGICAL PERIOD
Patriarchal Period	ca. 2000 BC to 1446 BC	*Middle Bronze Age*
Period of the Exodus	1446 BC to 1400 BC	*Late Bronze Age*
Period of Conquest	1400 BC to 1390 BC	
Period of the Judges	1390 BC to 1050 BC	*Late Bronze/Early Iron Age*
United Kingdom	1050 BC to 931 BC	*Iron Age*
Divided Kingdom	931 BC to 722 BC	
Single Kingdom	722 BC to 586 BC	
Babylonian Captivity	586 BC to 539 BC	
Restoration	539 BC to ca. 400 BC	*Persian Period*
Intertestamental Era	ca. 400 BC to 4 BC	*Hellenistic Period*
Life of Christ	4 BC to AD 33	*Roman Period*
Apostolic Age	AD 33 to ca. AD 70	

Beginning on the next page, each site in Israel is listed alphabetically. Following the description are key events of the appropriate historical periods and the main Scripture passages detailing those events.

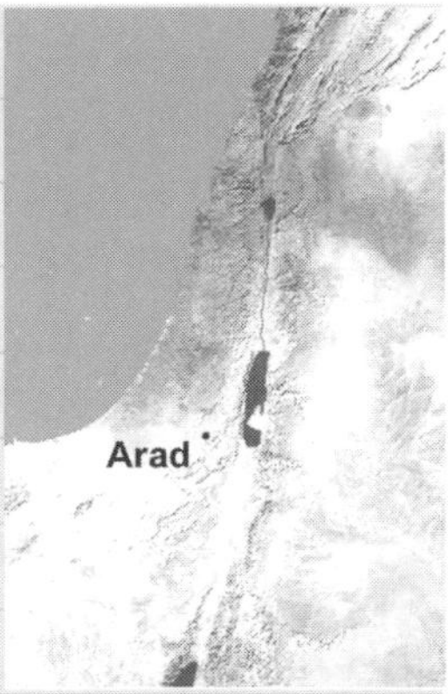

ARAD

The city of Arad, located in the eastern Negev basin, controlled the road from the hill country of Judah to Edom. A large city, with extensive fortifications, dominated the site in the Early Bronze Age. A smaller Iron Age fortress guarded the road and region at the end of the Judean monarchy. One of the most remarkable discoveries at the site was a complete temple patterned after God's temple in Jerusalem.

Period of the Exodus *Numbers 21:1–3*—The king of Arad attacked the Israelites toward the end of their time in the wilderness. Israel defeated the invaders and destroyed their cities, renaming the region Hormah ("destruction").

Period of Conquest *Judges 1:16*—The descendants of Moses' father-in-law, the Kenites, moved from Jericho to Arad and settled in the territory of Judah.

Reconstruction of the cultic temple of A

ASHKELON

Built on the Mediterranean Sea just twelve miles north of Gaza, Ashkelon is one of the five cities of the Philistines (along with Ashdod, Ekron, Gath, and Gaza). This city was also a great trading center because of its location along the International Highway, the major transportation route between Egypt and Mesopotamia. It is believed to be the birthplace of Herod the Great (in 37 BC) who later enlarged the city. Under the Romans, Ashkelon was granted the privilege of being exempt from taxes.

Period of Conquest *Judges 1:18*—After Joshua's death, Judah captured and controlled Ashkelon but was unable to hold it.

Period of the Judges *Judges 14:19*—Samson killed thirty men from Ashkelon and took their clothes to pay the wedding guests who had solved his riddle.

United Kingdom *1 Samuel 6:17*—Ashkelon was one of the Philistine cities that paid a guilt offering to God for their part in taking the ark of the covenant.

2 Samuel 1:20—David lamented over the deaths of Saul and Jonathan, asking that the tragic news not be proclaimed "in the streets of Ashkelon."

Divided Kingdom *Amos 1:8*—Amos denounced Ashkelon and three other Philistine cities for their sin of selling Israelites into slavery.

Overlooking the Mediterranean at As

Single Kingdom *Jeremiah 25:20; 47:5–7*—Jeremiah included Ashkelon in his list of cities and nations to be judged by God.

Zephaniah 2:4–7—Zephaniah predicted that the Jews would return from captivity to occupy Ashkelon and the other cities of the Philistines.

Restoration *Zechariah 9:5*—Zechariah predicted the conquest of Ashkelon and the other cities of the Philistines by Alexander the Great.

AZEKAH

The city of Azekah guarded the western edge of the Elah Valley. Strategically located on a high hill, the city stood on the border between Israel and the Philistines.

Period of Conquest *Joshua 10:10–11*—When Joshua attacked the Canaanite kings who threatened Gibeon, he pursued them "all the way to Azekah."

Joshua 15:35—God allotted Azekah to the tribe of Judah.

United Kingdom *1 Samuel 17:1*—When David fought Goliath, the battle took place in the Elah Valley. The Philistines camped on the southern side of the valley "between Socoh and Azekah."

Divided Kingdom *2 Chronicles 11:9*—King Rehoboam of Judah fortified Azekah as one of his cities of defense.

Single Kingdom *Jeremiah 34:7*—Nebuchadnezzar, king of Babylon, invaded Judah and sent his army against Judah's cities. Near the end of his invasion, only Lachish, Azekah, and Jerusalem remained unconquered. Eventually they all fell.

Restoration *Nehemiah 11:30*—Some of the remnant who returned from captivity in Babylon reinhabited Azekah.

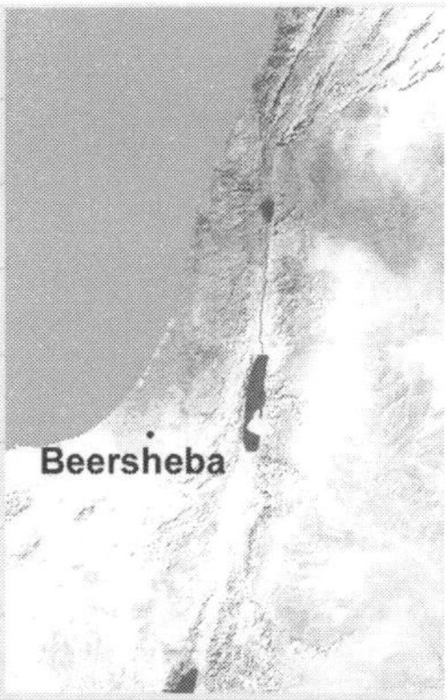

BEERSHEBA

The city of Beersheba was, practically speaking, the southernmost city of Israel in the Old Testament. When the writers of Scripture wanted to speak of all Israel (from north to south), they would say "from Dan to Beersheba" (Judg. 20:1; 1 Sam. 3:20; 2 Sam. 3:10; 17:11; 24:2, 15; 1 Kings 4:25). Beersheba controlled the central Negev basin.

Patriarchal Period *Genesis 21:14*—When Hagar and Ishmael were forced to leave Abraham's camp, they wandered in the wilderness of Beersheba.

Genesis 21:25–34—Abraham made an agreement, paid seven ewe lambs, and took an oath with Abimelech to establish ownership over a well Abraham had dug. The place was named Beersheba ("well of the oath" or "well of seven").

Genesis 26:26–33—Isaac also quarreled with Abimelech and took an oath. That same day his servants found water, and Isaac named the place Beersheba ("well of the oath").

Well of Beersheba

Genesis 28:10—Jacob stole the birthright from Esau while the family camped at Beersheba. He then left Beersheba to travel to Haran to find a wife.

Genesis 46:1–7—Jacob paused at Beersheba to offer sacrifices before leaving the Promised Land for Egypt.

Period of Conquest *Joshua 15:28; 19:2*—Beersheba was located in the territory given to the tribe of Judah. But God allotted the city to the tribe of Simeon, who had their inheritance scattered among the tribe of Judah.

1 Samuel 8:1–2—Samuel's sons judged Israel in Beersheba.

Divided Kingdom *1 Kings 19:1–4*—Elijah stopped at Beersheba as he fled from Jezebel. He left his servant there, but he continued to flee south for another day.

Single Kingdom *2 Kings 23:8*—Under King Josiah's reforms, the high place inside the city of Beersheba was torn down.

Restoration *Nehemiah 11:27*—Some of the remnant who returned from captivity in Babylon reinhabited Beersheba.

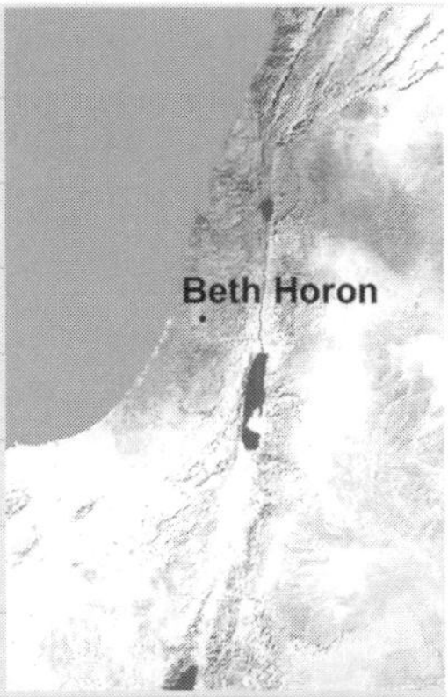

BETH HORON

Two villages, Upper Beth Horon and Lower Beth Horon, straddled the ridge that extends from the Aijalon Valley to the hill country just north of Jerusalem. These towns guarded the main road from the Mediterranean coast to Jerusalem.

Period of Conquest *Joshua 10:9–14*—Joshua chased the Canaanites along the "road down from Beth Horon to Azekah" when he rescued Gibeon.

Joshua 16:1–5; 18:13–14—Beth Horon was on the border between the tribes of Benjamin and Ephraim.

Joshua 21:20–22—God allotted Beth Horon to the Levites as one of their forty-eight cities of inheritance throughout the land of Israel.

United Kingdom *1 Samuel 13:17–18*—The Philistines sent raiding parties along the road at Beth Horon when they threatened Israel during the days of King Saul.

1 Kings 9:17; 2 Chronicles 8:5—Solomon fortified Beth Horon to protect the main road to Jerusalem.

Divided Kingdom *2 Chronicles 25:13*—Troops of Amaziah, king of Judah, rioted and raided cities of Judah from Beth Horon to Samaria when they were sent home from battle.

BETH SHAN/SCYTHOPOLIS

Beth Shan is located at the strategic juncture of the Jezreel and Jordan Valleys. Like Jericho, Beth Shan was almost continuously occupied throughout history. During the intertestamental period, the city was renamed Scythopolis. Today archaeologists are uncovering the extensive ruins of Roman/Byzantine Scythopolis.

Period of Conquest *Joshua 17:11, 16; Judges 1:27*—God allotted Beth Shan to the tribe of Manasseh, but they were unable to drive out the Canaanites because "all the Canaanites who live in the plain have iron chariots, both those in Beth Shan and its settlements and those in the Valley of Jezreel" (Josh. 17:16).

United Kingdom *1 Samuel 31:10–12*—After defeating Saul and his sons on Mount Gilboa, the Philistines hanged their bodies on the walls of Beth Shan.

1 Kings 4:12—Solomon placed Beth Shan, Megiddo, and Jezreel under the governorship of Baana, son of Ahilud.

Life of Christ Scythopolis was one of the chief cities of the Decapolis—a league of ten cities sharing Greek culture and government.

Tel Beth Shan, the site of the Old Testament city, with the Roman city in the foreground

BETH SHEMESH

Beth Shemesh ("house of the sun") sits at the eastern end of the Sorek Valley. This city, assigned to the Levites, marked the historical border between Israel and the Philistines.

Period of Conquest *Joshua 15:10*—Beth Shemesh was on the border between the tribes of Judah and Dan.

Joshua 21:16—God allotted Beth Shemesh to the Levites as one of their forty-eight cities of inheritance throughout the land of Israel.

Period of the Judges *Judges 13–16*—Samson was a Danite who lived in the Sorek Valley near Beth Shemesh. Zorah, Eshtaol, and Timnah are all near Beth Shemesh.

1 Samuel 6:7–21—When the Philistines returned the ark of the covenant to the Israelites, it went by cart to Beth Shemesh. Some Israelites were killed when they looked inside the ark, so the people of Beth Shemesh refused to let the ark stay in their town.

Divided Kingdom *2 Kings 14:11–14; 2 Chronicles 25:21–24*—King Amaziah of Judah was defeated and captured by King Jehoash of Israel at Beth Shemesh. The army of Israel then went to Jerusalem and tore down sections of the city wall.

2 Chronicles 28:16–18—The Philistines captured Beth Shemesh during the reign of King Ahaz. Ahaz appealed to the Assyrians for help in recapturing this city.

BETHANY

Bethany was a small village on the east slope of the Mount of Olives, about two miles from Jerusalem. Jesus often spent the night in Bethany during His visits to Jerusalem.

Life of Christ *John 11:1*—Mary, Martha, and Lazarus lived in Bethany.

Matthew 21:17; Mark 11:11; Luke 10:38–42—Jesus stayed in Bethany when He visited Jerusalem. Here Mary sat at Jesus' feet while Martha was serving.

John 11:1–44—Jesus raised Lazarus from the dead in Bethany. Today the city's Arabic name is El-Azariyeh, preserving the town's connection to Lazarus.

Matthew 26:6–13; Mark 14:3–9; John 12:1–8—In the house of Simon the leper, Mary anointed Jesus with expensive ointment.

Mark 11:1–11; Luke 19:29–40—Between Bethany and Bethphage, Jesus asked two of His disciples to get a donkey and a colt for His triumphal entry.

Matthew 21:18–22; Mark 11:12–14—Jesus cursed a fruitless fig tree here, and it withered.

Luke 24:50–53—Jesus ascended to heaven from the Mount of Olives near "the vicinity of Bethany."

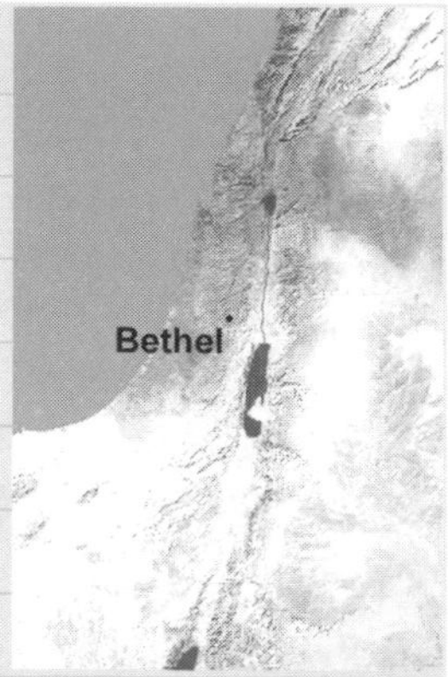

BETHEL

Bethel ("house of God"), a strategic village in the hill country of Israel, sat on the internal north–south road from Shechem to Beersheba, where that road intersected another road coming into the hill country from Jericho. Bethel played a major role in Israel's religious history.

Patriarchal Period *Genesis 12:8; 13:3*—Abram camped near Bethel and built an altar to the Lord.

Genesis 28:10–22—On his journey to Haran, Jacob camped at Bethel and had a vision of angels ascending and descending a stairway between earth and heaven.

Genesis 35:1–15—Jacob returned to Bethel and built an altar to God.

Period of Conquest *Joshua 8:10–17; 12:16*—The men of Bethel joined forces with the men of Ai to fight against Israel. Israel evidently captured Bethel when they defeated Ai.

Joshua 16:1–2; 18:13, 22—Although Bethel rested on the border between the tribes of Ephraim and Benjamin, God allotted Bethel to Benjamin.

Period of the Judges *Judges 1:22–26*—The "house of Joseph" (Ephraim) captured Bethel and claimed it for themselves.

Judges 4:4–5—The prophetess/judge Deborah held court between Ramah and Bethel.

1 Samuel 7:16—Samuel included Bethel on the circuit of cities from which he judged Israel.

Divided Kingdom *1 Kings 12:26–33*—Jeroboam, the first king of the northern kingdom of Israel, set up golden calves in Dan and Bethel to keep the people from going to Jerusalem to worship.

1 Kings 13:1–6—Jeroboam's hand was temporarily shriveled when he opposed a prophet sent by God to condemn the false worship at Bethel.

2 Kings 2:23–24—A group of young men from Bethel were mauled by bears when they mocked the prophet Elisha.

Hosea 10:15; Amos 4:4; 9:1–2—The prophets Hosea and Amos predicted the destruction of the temple of Bethel and the captivity of Israel.

Amos 7:10–17—The high priest at Bethel rejected the message of Amos and brought God's judgment on his own household as a result.

Single Kingdom *2 Kings 23:15–16*—King Josiah of Judah destroyed the temple and defiled the altar at Bethel set up by Jeroboam.

Restoration *Ezra 2:28; Nehemiah 7:32; 11:31*—Some of the remnant who returned from captivity in Babylon reinhabited Bethel.

BETHLEHEM

Bethlehem ("house of bread") was originally a small village just to the east of the main road through the hill country of Judah. The village received enough rainfall to support agriculture, but it was also close enough to the Judean Wilderness to encourage the raising of sheep and goats.

Patriarchal Period *Genesis 35:16–20; 48:7*—The tomb of Rachel, wife of Jacob and mother of Joseph and Benjamin, is just outside Bethlehem. Rachel died while giving birth to Benjamin.

Period of the Judges *Book of Ruth*—The story of Ruth and Boaz took place here during the barley and wheat harvest.

United Kingdom *1 Samuel 16:1–13; 17:12*—David was born in Bethlehem and anointed here by Samuel as king of Israel. David was called from tending his father's flocks to shepherd the nation of Israel.

1 Samuel 17:15, 34–37—Although David was a shepherd in Bethlehem, he

Looking south toward modern-day Bethlehem

traveled to the Valley of Elah where he killed Goliath (1 Sam. 17:12–58).

2 Samuel 23:13–17—While fleeing from King Saul, David longed for water from the well at Bethlehem.

Divided Kingdom *Micah 5:2*—Micah prophesied that the Messiah would be born in the village of Bethlehem.

Life of Christ *Luke 2:1–7*—In fulfillment of the prophecy of Micah 5:2, Jesus was born in Bethlehem.

Luke 2:8–20—The shepherds visited the infant Jesus in Bethlehem.

Matthew 2:1–12—The wise men, led by the star, visited and worshiped the infant "king of the Jews" in Bethlehem.

Matthew 2:13–18—Joseph fled with Mary and Jesus to Egypt to avoid the cruelty of Herod, who killed all the babies of Bethlehem two years old and under in a vain attempt to destroy the Lord's Messiah.

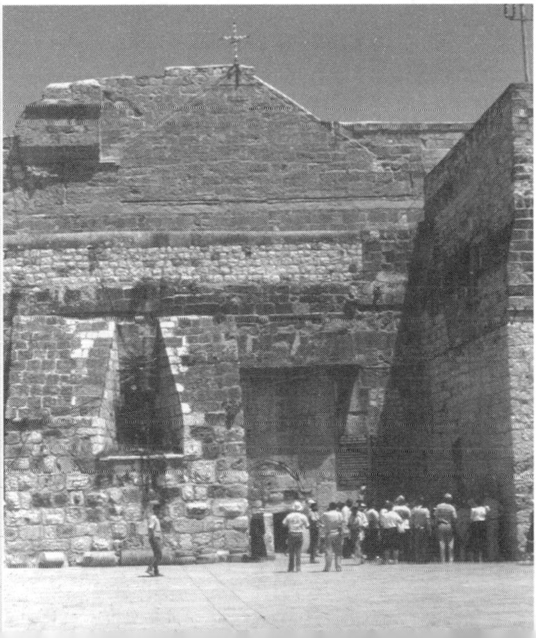

Entrance to the Church of the Nativity in Bethlehem

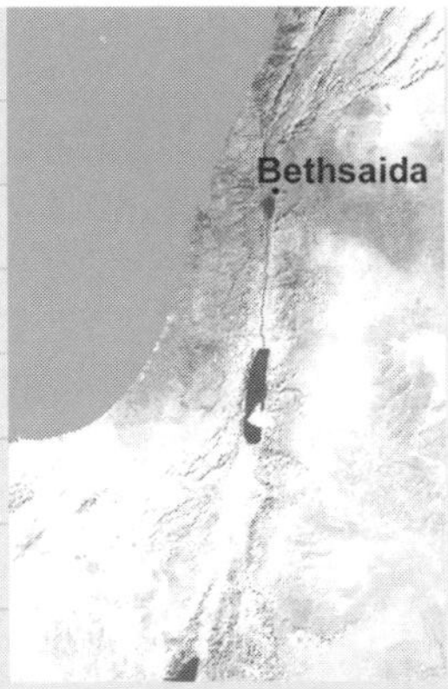

BETHSAIDA

Bethsaida ("house of fishing") was a town east of the Jordan River and just north of the Sea of Galilee. Philip the Tetrarch extensively rebuilt Bethsaida and renamed it "Julias" after Julia, the daughter of Augustus Caesar.

Life of Christ *Matthew 11:20–22*—Jesus rebuked Bethsaida for refusing to repent in spite of the miracles He performed there.

Mark 8:22–26—Jesus healed a blind man outside Bethsaida.

Luke 9:10–17—Jesus fed the five thousand near Bethsaida.

John 1:44—Bethsaida was the hometown of the apostles Peter, Andrew, and Philip.

Plain of Bethsaida on the northeastern shore of the Sea of Gali

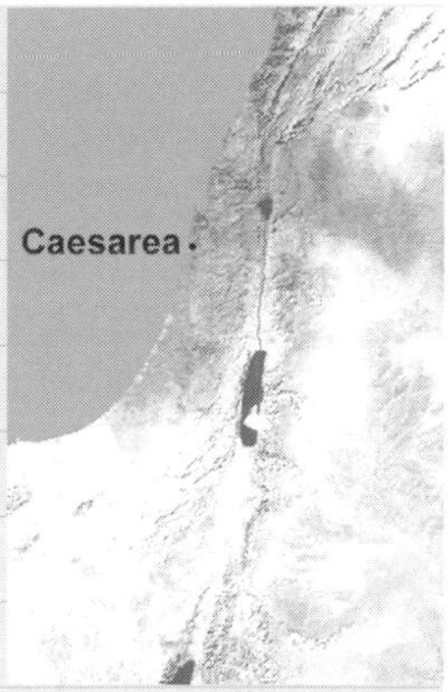

CAESAREA

Caesarea was originally a poor harbor on the Mediterranean coast that was called Strato's Tower. The city of Caesarea was founded by Herod the Great in 22 BC and was the seat of the Roman government for over five hundred years. Herod completely rebuilt the city and named it Caesarea in honor of Augustus Caesar. Caesarea was the home of the Roman procurators, including Pontius Pilate, whose name was discovered here on an inscription that identified him as the "prefect of Judah." The existing walls and gate of

The Herodian aqueduct brought water to the city of Caesarea.

the harbor were built in the time of the Crusades (twelfth century AD). The theater and aqueduct were built by Herod the Great and later modified by the Romans in the second century AD.

Apostolic Age *Acts 8:40; 21:8–9*—Philip, one of the seven "deacons" in Jerusalem (Acts 6:5), was the first to preach in Caesarea. He settled there and had four daughters who prophesied.

Acts 10—Peter came to Caesarea in response to a vision at Joppa and preached the gospel in Cornelius's home. The Holy Spirit was poured out as at Pentecost, showing that the door of the gospel was now open to the Gentiles.

Acts 12:19–24—God struck down Herod Agrippa I in Caesarea for accepting the worship of others who called him a god and for persecuting the early church.

Acts 9:30; 18:22; 21:8–16—Paul visited the city three times, and on the third occasion he was warned that if he went to Jerusalem, he would be captured by the Jews and delivered to the Gentiles.

Acts 23:23–27:2—Paul spent two years in prison in Caesarea. He made his defense in three outstanding addresses before Felix and Festus (Roman governors or procurators) and before King Herod Agrippa II.

Performances are once again held at the restored Herodian theater at Caesare

CAESAREA PHILIPPI

Caesarea Philippi was originally called Panion or Panias after the Greek god Pan. Herod the Great's son, Philip, established it as the capital of his tetrarchy and named it Caesarea to honor the emperor of Rome. It was known as Caesarea Philippi ("Philip's Caesarea"), to distinguish it from other cities with the same name.

Intertestamental Era Antiochus III of Syria defeated the Egyptians at Panias in 197 BC and took control of the region. This control by the Seleucid dynasty set the stage for the oppression of the Jews by Antiochus IV and the revolt of the Maccabees.

Life of Christ *Matthew 16:13; Mark 8:27*— Caesarea Philippi marks the northernmost limit of Christ's ministry.

Matthew 16:13–16; Mark 8:27–30; Luke 9:18–21— Peter made his confession of Christ's deity in response to Jesus' question, "Who do people say the Son of Man is?" in the region of Caesarea Philippi.

Stone niche carved into the rock, in which the statue of a pagan god was placed

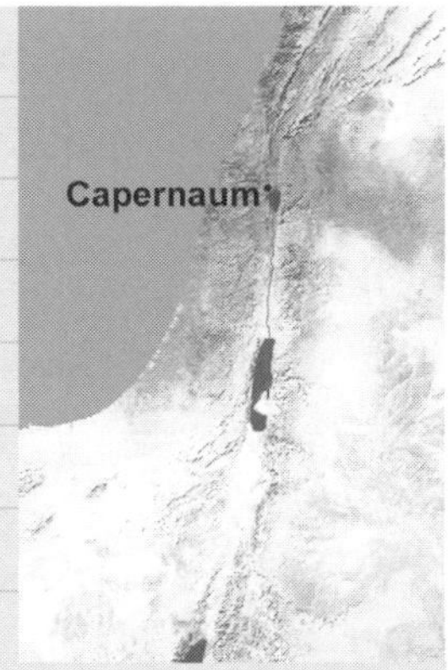

CAPERNAUM

Capernaum was an important town in the time of Christ because it was located on the Sea of Galilee (and had access to the fishing industry there) and because it straddled the International Highway, which went from Mesopotamia to Egypt, at one of its narrowest points. Thus Capernaum controlled trade along this important highway. Its prominence is indicated by the presence of a Roman centurion and detachment of troops (Matt. 8:5–9), a customs station (Matt. 9:9), and a high officer of the king (John 4:46).

Remains of the ancient synagogue at Capernau

Life of Christ *Matthew 4:13–16*—Rejected at Nazareth, Jesus moved to Capernaum and made it the center of His activity for eighteen to twenty months.

Matthew 4:18–22; Mark 1:16–21—

Peter, Andrew, James, and John were called to be disciples near Capernaum.

Matthew 9:9–13; Mark 2:14—Jesus called Matthew (Levi) from the office of the Capernaum tax or tollhouse to be His disciple. (Tolls were collected on the traffic from Mesopotamia and Damascus through Capernaum to the coast and Egypt.)

Mark 1:21–34; Luke 4:31–41—Jesus taught in the synagogue at Capernaum, delivered a man from an unclean spirit, and also healed Peter's mother-in-law as well as many others.

Matthew 8:5–13; Luke 7:1–10—Jesus healed the centurion's servant. Capernaum was a Roman military center, and this Roman centurion helped fund the construction of the Jewish synagogue in Capernaum.

Matthew 9:1–8; Mark 2:1–12; Luke 5:17–26—A paralyzed man was let down through the roof and healed by Jesus in Capernaum.

Matthew 9:18–26; Mark 5:22–43; Luke 8:40–56—In Capernaum, Jesus raised Jairus's daughter from the dead and healed the woman who had a hemorrhage.

John 4:46–54—Jesus also healed the nobleman's son in Capernaum.

Matthew 9:27–35; 12:22–45; Mark 3:20–22; Luke 11:14–26—Two blind men and a mute demoniac were healed in Capernaum.

Matthew 8:16–17; 9:36–38—Many sick people were brought to Jesus and healed in Capernaum. In fact, more of Christ's recorded miracles were performed in Capernaum than in any other city. Yet Capernaum did not believe (Matt. 11:23–24)

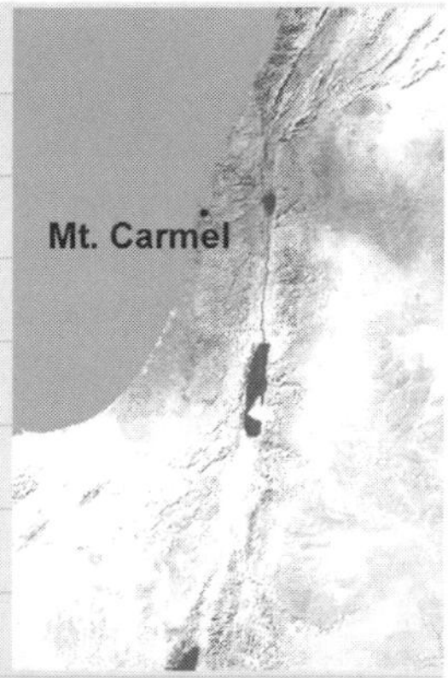

CARMEL (MOUNT)

Mount Carmel is a wooded mountain range, triangular in shape, thirteen miles long, projecting into the Mediterranean Sea at Haifa. The mountain rises from the sea so sharply that the rapidly rising air deposits its moisture as rain or dew. Thus the mountain is lush year-round. Only a catastrophic drought would cause Mount Carmel to turn brown and wither. From antiquity, altars to strange gods were erected on its heights, and it was, particularly, a sanctuary for the worship of Baal.

United Kingdom *Song of Songs 7:5*—Solomon compared the stately majesty of his bride's head to the summit of Carmel.

Divided Kingdom *1 Kings 18:19–39*—Elijah had his contest with the prophets of Baal on Mount Carmel.

1 Kings 18:40—Elijah killed the prophets of Baal at the foot of Mount Carmel, at the Brook Kishon.

1 Kings 18:42–46—Elijah prayed on the top of Mount Carmel and announced that the three-and-a-half-year drought would end. He then outran Ahab's chariot from Mount Carmel to Jezreel.

Isaiah 35:2—Isaiah used Mount Carmel as a symbol of beauty, fruitfulness, majesty, and glory.

Isaiah 33:9; Amos 1:2; Nahum 1:4—When Carmel is referred to as languishing and withering, it indicates God's judgment on His land.

Single Kingdom *Jeremiah 46:18*—Jeremiah compared the grandeur of Nebuchadnezzar to the exalted height of Mount Carmel and Mount Tabor.

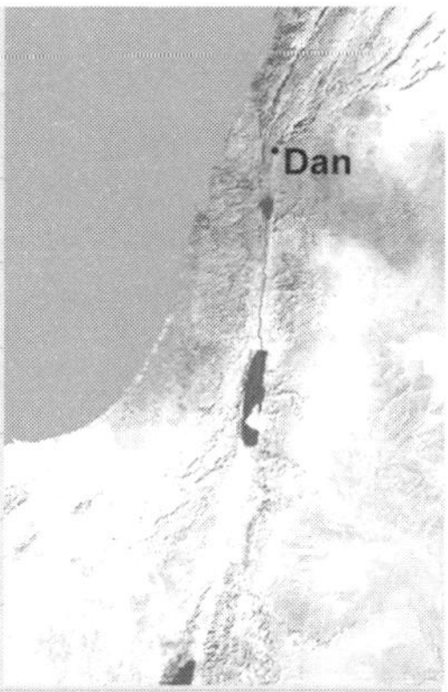

DAN

The city of Dan was, practically speaking, the northernmost city of Israel in the Old Testament. When the writers of Scripture wanted to speak of all Israel (from north to south), they would say "from Dan to Beersheba" (Judg. 20:1; 1 Sam. 3:20; 2 Sam. 3:10; 17:11; 24:2, 15; 1 Kings 4:25).

Patriarchal Period *Genesis 14:13–16*—Abram traveled from Hebron to Dan to rescue his nephew Lot from Kedorlaomer.

Period of the Judges *Judges 18*—The tribe of Dan was not satisfied with its allotted inheritance near Judah and so settled here, both giving its name to the region and setting up idolatrous worship that plagued Israel throughout its history.

Divided Kingdom *1 Kings 12:26–33*—Jeroboam, the first king of the northern kingdom of Israel, set up golden calves in Dan and Bethel to keep the people from going to Jerusalem to worship.

Single Kingdom *Jeremiah 4:15; 8:15–16*—The city of Dan symbolized the northern edge of the land, the "gateway" through which Judah's enemies would pass on their way to Jerusalem.

Platform in the city gate at Dan where the ruler would sit to judge

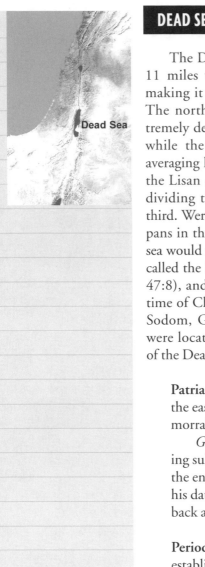

DEAD SEA

The Dead Sea is approximately 45 miles long, 11 miles wide, and 1,350 feet below sea level, making it the lowest point on the earth's surface. The northern two-thirds of the Dead Sea is extremely deep, reaching a depth of over 1,200 feet, while the southern third is extremely shallow, averaging less than 20 feet. A tongue of land called the Lisan cuts across the Dead Sea from the east, dividing the northern section from the southern third. Were water not being channeled into the salt pans in the south, the entire southern third of the sea would now be dry. In the Bible, the Dead Sea is called the Salt Sea (Num. 34:3, 12), the Sea (Ezek. 47:8), and the eastern sea (Joel 2:20). During the time of Christ, it was also called Lake Asphaltitus. Sodom, Gomorrah, and the "cities of the plain" were located in and around the southern portion of the Dead Sea.

Patriarchal Period *Genesis 14:3*—The kings of the east defeated the kings of Sodom and Gomorrah "in the Valley of Siddim (the Salt Sea)."

Genesis 18–19—God "rained down burning sulfur on Sodom and Gomorrah . . . and the entire plain." Abraham's nephew Lot and his daughters escaped, but Lot's wife looked back and became a pillar of salt.

Period of the Exodus *Numbers 34:3, 12*—God established the Salt Sea as part of Israel's eastern border.

United Kingdom *1 Samuel 22:3–5*—David likely crossed the Dead Sea on the Lisan when he took his family from Judah to Moab to protect them from King Saul. David returned and stayed at "the stronghold" (possibly Masada).

Divided Kingdom *2 Chronicles 20*—A combined army from Ammon, Moab, and Edom crossed the Dead Sea at the Lisan to launch a surprise attack against Jerusalem and King Jehoshaphat. God intervened to spare Jerusalem.

Joel 2:20—God promised to remove the locusts (the "northern army") from the land, pushing them into "the eastern sea" (the Dead Sea) and "the western sea" (the Mediterranean Sea).

Single Kingdom *Jeremiah 17:6*—Jeremiah compared those who trusted in human alliances, rather than God, to a bush dwelling near the Dead Sea in "the parched places of the desert, in a salt land where no one lives."

Babylonian Captivity *Ezekiel 47:8–11*—Ezekiel predicted a time when the Dead Sea would become fresh and when fishermen would line its banks.

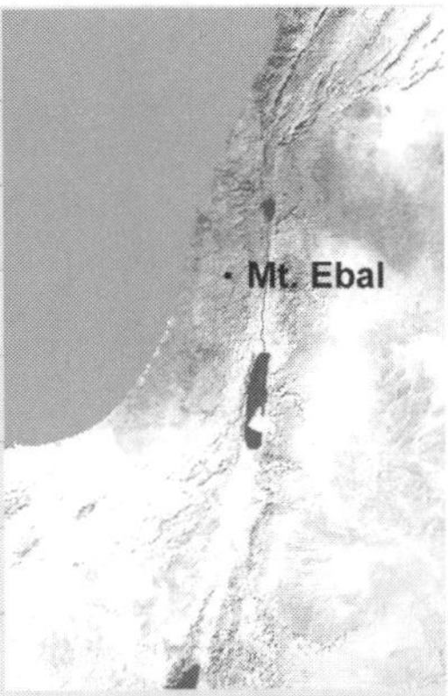

EBAL (MOUNT)

Mount Ebal, rising nearly 3,100 feet above sea level, sits on the northern side of the biblical city of Shechem (modern Nablus). With its twin peak, Mount Gerizim, to the south, these two mountains form a natural valley that leads west from Shechem toward the Mediterranean coast. Mount Ebal is known as the mount of cursing because the curses of God's law were recited from its slopes. For more information see Gerizim (Mount) and Shechem.

Period of the Exodus *Deuteronomy 11:29*—God commanded Israel to travel to Mount Ebal and Mount Gerizim to recite the blessings and cursings of the covenant once they entered the Promised Land. The cursings were to be recited from Mount Ebal.

Deuteronomy 27:1–8—God commanded Israel to build an altar and set up pillars inscribed with the words of His law on Mount Ebal.

Period of Conquest *Joshua 8:30–35*—Joshua led the Israelites to Mount Ebal and Mount Gerizim to recite the blessings and cursings of the law as God had commanded. Joshua also built the altar and set up the pillars inscribed with the words of the law on Mount Ebal.

Life of Christ *John 4:4–6*—The "woman at the well" whom Jesus met in Samaria was from the village of Sychar located on the slopes of Mount Ebal.

ELAH VALLEY

The Elah Valley gets its name from the terebinth tree (Hebrew *elah*), which can still be found there. These trees have a very extensive root system and can grow quite large. The valley itself is one of the five major valleys running east–west through the foothills between the coastal plain and the hill country of Judah. The Elah Valley begins just to the east of Gath and ends at a ridge that leads to Bethlehem. The principal towns in this valley during the biblical period were Socoh and Azekah.

United Kingdom *1 Samuel 17:2, 19; 21:9*— David defeated Goliath in the Elah Valley after a forty-day standoff between the armies of Israel and the Philistines.

The streambed where David paused to pick up his five smooth stones still cuts through the Elah Valley.

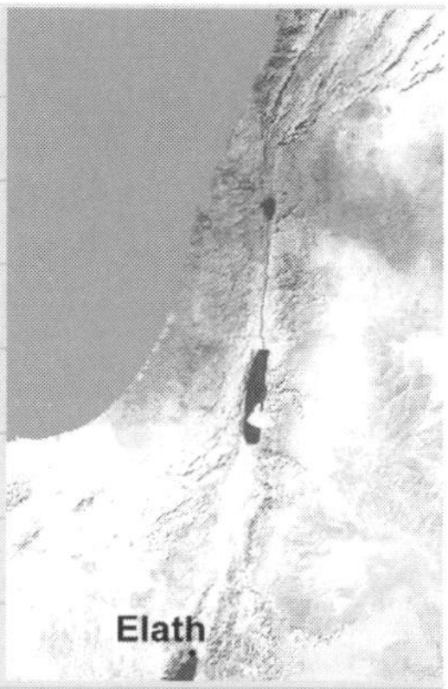

ELATH/EZION GEBER

Elath was a coastal city at the northern end of the eastern finger of the Red Sea that jutted up from the Sinai peninsula. Elath and the adjacent city of Ezion Geber served as port cities for trade with the Arabian peninsula and Africa. Israel's modern city of Eilat is located in this same area today.

Period of the Exodus *Numbers 33:35–36; Deuteronomy 2:8*—Israel traveled by Elath and Ezion Geber as they circled around the land of Edom on their way to the east of the Jordan River.

United Kingdom *1 Kings 9:26–28; 2 Chronicles 8:17–18*—King Solomon built a fleet of ships at Ezion Geber to sail to Ophir.

Divided Kingdom *1 Kings 22:48; 2 Chronicles 20:35–37*—King Jehoshaphat built a fleet of ships at Ezion Geber to sail to Ophir, but they were destroyed.

2 Kings 14:22; 2 Chronicles 26:1–2—King Azariah (Uzziah) recaptured Elath and restored it to Judah's control.

2 Kings 16:6—King Rezin of Aram conquered Elath and drove Judah out.

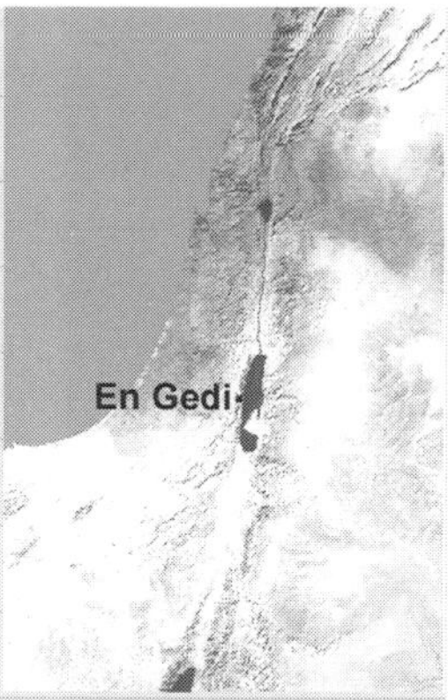

EN GEDI

En Gedi ("spring of the wild goat") is an oasis in the Judean Wilderness on the western shore of the Dead Sea. Because of its warm climate and abundant supply of water, the site developed a reputation for its fragrant plants and date palm groves.

Period of Conquest *Joshua 15:62*—God allotted En Gedi to the tribe of Judah.

United Kingdom *1 Samuel 23:29*—David hid in a cave at En Gedi when running from Saul.

1 Samuel 24—Saul entered the cave where David and his men were hiding, and David cut off part of Saul's robe while Saul "relieve[d] himself."

Psalms 57; 142—These psalms may have been composed here by David.

Song of Songs 1:14—Solomon's beloved compared him to "a cluster of henna blossoms" growing in the vineyards of En Gedi.

Divided Kingdom *2 Chronicles 20:1–30*—The Moabites, Ammonites, and Edomites united together at En Gedi to launch a surprise attack against Jerusalem. (En Gedi is the "back door" to Jerusalem from the Dead Sea.) God miraculously intervened to have these nations attack each other instead of Jerusalem.

Ezekiel 47:10—Someday in the future, fishermen will line the shores of the Dead Sea "from En Gedi to En Eglaim" to fish.

GALILEE (SEA OF)

The Sea of Galilee is 13 miles long, 7 1/2 miles wide at its northern end, 130–157 feet deep, 32 miles in circumference, and 650 feet below sea level. In the Bible it is called the Sea of Kinnereth (Num. 34:11; Deut. 3:17; Josh. 13:27; 19:35), the Lake of Gennesaret (Luke 5:1), the Sea of Tiberias (John 21:1), and the Sea of Galilee (Matt. 4:18; 15:29; Mark 1:16; 7:31; John 6:1). Technically, this body of water should be more properly described as a lake than a sea.

View from the Mount of Beatitudes toward Mount Arbe

Period of Conquest *Numbers 34:11*—The mountain range on the eastern shore of the Sea of Kinnereth (Sea of Galilee) was to be the eastern boundary of the Promised Land.

Life of Christ *Luke 5:4–11; John 21:6–8*—The Sea of Galilee yielded two large catches of fish in response to the command of Christ.

Matthew 8:1–4—Jesus healed a leper near the Sea of Galilee as He came down from a mountain on His way to Capernaum.

Matthew 8:23–27; Mark 4:35–41; Luke 8:22–25—Jesus stilled the storm on the Sea of Galilee.

Matthew 8:28–34; Mark 5:1–21; Luke 8:26–39—Demons, cast out of the demoniac by Christ, entered two thousand swine, which plunged into the Sea of Galilee from a steep bank on the eastern shore.

Matthew 14:22–33; Mark 6:45–52; John 6:16–21—Jesus walked on the water to the disciples who were struggling in their boat.

Matthew 18:1–6—Jesus said it would be better to have a millstone tied around one's neck and be drowned in the sea than to cause one who believed in Him to sin. Since Jesus spoke these words in Capernaum (Matt. 17:24), the "sea" He spoke of was likely the Sea of Galilee.

John 21—Jesus met the disciples on the shore of the Sea of Galilee after His resurrection.

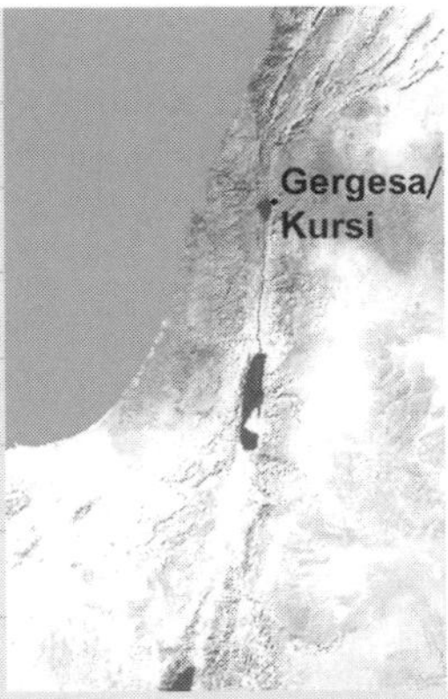

GERGESA/KURSI

This uninhabited location on the eastern shore of the Sea of Galilee is the site of the largest known Byzantine monastery in Israel. The monastery, along with a smaller chapel just up the hill, were built to commemorate the place where Jesus cast the demons out of the man who lived among the tombs and into a herd of swine.

The first three Gospels provide different names for the location where the miracle took place. Matthew records one location while Mark and Luke record another. It seems likely that Matthew—writing to a Jewish audience—recorded the specific town where the event happened, while Mark and Luke—writing for Roman and Greek audiences, respectively—recorded the nearest city recognizable to readers unfamiliar with the region.

Life of Christ *Matthew 8:28; Mark 5:1; Luke 8:26*—After crossing the Sea of Galilee during a storm, Jesus heals the demoniac by casting out the demons into a herd of swine.

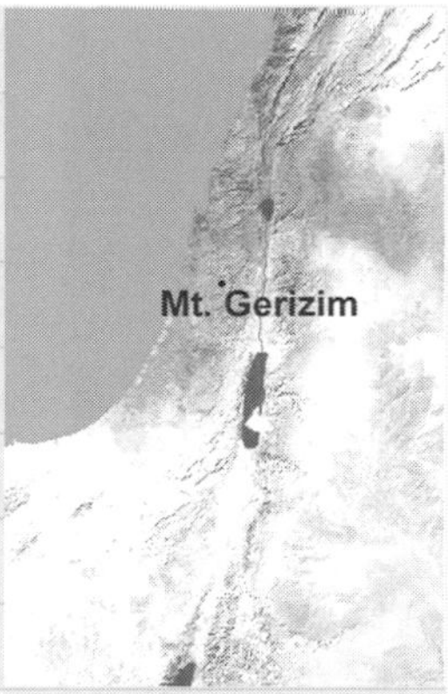

GERIZIM (MOUNT)

Mount Gerizim, at 2,900 feet above sea level, stands slightly lower than its counterpart to the north, Mount Ebal. Both tower over the biblical city of Shechem (modern Nablus). These two mountains form a natural valley that leads west from Shechem to the Mediterranean coast. Mount Gerizim is known as the mount of blessing because the blessings of God's law were recited from its slopes. During the intertestamental period, the Samaritans erected a temple on Mount Gerizim to rival the Jewish temple in Jerusalem. The Jewish leader John Hyrcanus destroyed the Samaritan temple in 129 BC. This fueled the continuing animosity between the Jews and the Samaritans. For more information see Ebal (Mount) and Shechem.

Looking up at Mount Gerizim from Jacob's well

Period of the Exodus *Deuteronomy 11:29*—God commanded Israel to travel to Mount Ebal and Mount Gerizim to recite the blessings and cursings of the covenant once they entered the Promised Land. The blessings were to be recited from Mount Gerizim.

Deuteronomy 27:12–13—God identified the tribes who were to stand on Mount Ebal and those who were to stand on Mount Gerizim to recite the blessings and cursings.

Period of Conquest *Joshua 8:30–35*—Joshua led the Israelites to Mount Ebal and Mount Gerizim to recite the blessings and cursings of the law as God had commanded.

Period of the Judges *Judges 9:1–21*—Gideon's youngest son, Jotham, stood on Mount Gerizim and delivered a message condemning the city of Shechem for making his one brother king and condoning the killing of his other brothers.

Life of Christ *John 4:19–24*—The "woman at the well" whom Jesus met in Samaria pointed to Mount Gerizim when she declared, "Our fathers worshiped on this mountain."

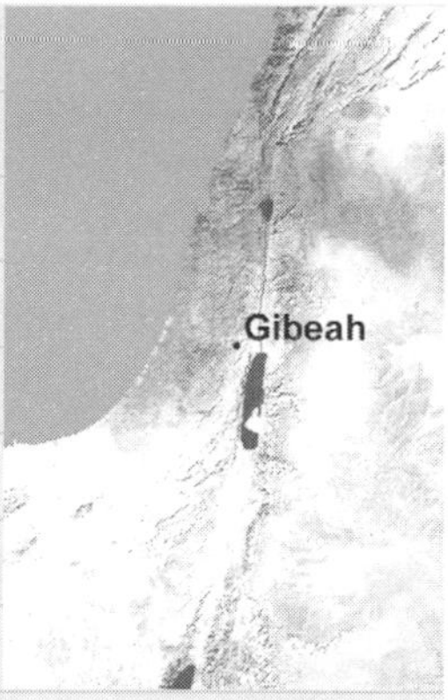

GIBEAH

Gibeah, today a hill called Tell el-Ful, was located just three miles north of ancient Jerusalem. The city received its dubious reputation because of its immorality (which started the Benjamite war in the book of Judges) and because it was the hometown of King Saul, Israel's first king, who was rejected by God.

Period of Conquest *Joshua 18:28*—Gibeah was assigned to the tribe of Benjamin.

Period of the Judges *Judges 19:10–26*—The men of Gibeah raped and killed a Levite's concubine, bringing shame on the nation.

Judges 20:1–48—The tribe of Benjamin was nearly wiped out from the civil war that resulted when the Benjamites refused to turn over the men of Gibeah who had sinned.

United Kingdom *1 Samuel 10:26; 11:4*—Saul, Israel's first king, came from Gibeah. After his anointing as king, the city was known as "Gibeah of Saul."

1 Samuel 13:2, 15; 14:2, 16—During his early conflicts with the Philistines, Saul frequently positioned his forces in or near Gibeah.

2 Samuel 21:4–9—David allowed the Gibeonites to kill seven sons of Saul in Gibeah because of Saul's treachery against them.

Single Kingdom *Isaiah 10:31; Hosea 5:8*—The inhabitants of Gibeah fled their village when the Assyrian army marched on Jerusalem in 701 BC. Gibeah fell to the Assyrians.

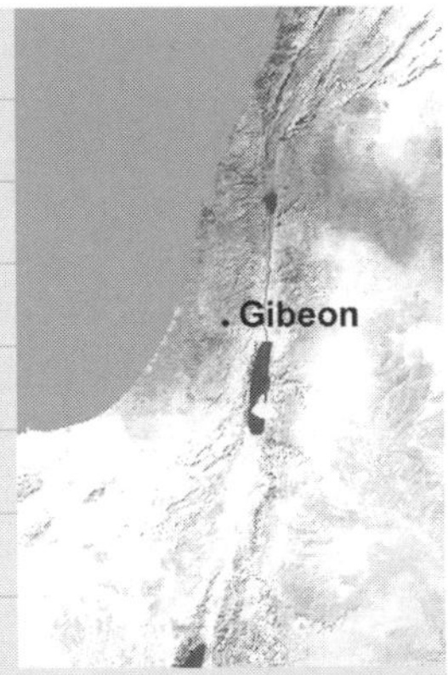

GIBEON

Ancient Gibeon watched over the upper end of the main road from the coastal plain into the hill country. The city, while under Israelite control, was inhabited by the Hivites, who had tricked Joshua into making a peace treaty with them. The modern Arab village of El-Jib preserves the name of ancient Gibeon.

Period of Conquest *Joshua 9–10*—The Gibeonites tricked Joshua into making a peace treaty with them, thus allowing them to live in the land as Israel's servants. Five kings of southern Canaan attacked Gibeon when they heard of the Gibeonite treaty with Israel. Joshua marched his army from Gilgal, attacked the armies that had surrounded Gibeon, and defeated them.

Joshua 21:17—Gibeon and the surrounding land was allotted to the Levites as one of their forty-eight cities in the land of Israel.

United Kingdom *2 Samuel 2:12–17*—Joab and David's forces met Abner and Ishbosheth's forces at the pool of Gibeon, and David's men won.

2 Samuel 21:4–9—David allowed the Gibeonites to kill seven sons of Saul in Gibeah because of Saul's treachery against them.

1 Kings 3:4; 2 Chronicles 1:3–13—After becoming king, Solomon offered sacrifices to the Lord at Gibeon and asked for wisdom. God promised him wisdom as well as riches and honor.

1 Chronicles 16:37–43; 21:28–30—The tabernacle of the Lord was at Gibeon before Solomon constructed the temple in Jerusalem. (This explains why Solomon went to Gibeon to worship in 1 Kings 3:4.)

Single Kingdom *Jeremiah 28:1*—Hananiah, the false prophet who opposed Jeremiah, was from Gibeon.

Babylonian Captivity *Jeremiah 41:11–12*—Jeremiah and the other captives from Mizpah were rescued by the pool of Gibeon.

Restoration *Nehemiah 3:7; 7:25*—Ninety-five men returned from the Babylonian captivity to their ancestral home in Gibeon. They also helped rebuild the walls of Jerusalem.

The site of ancient Gibeon from Nebi Samwil

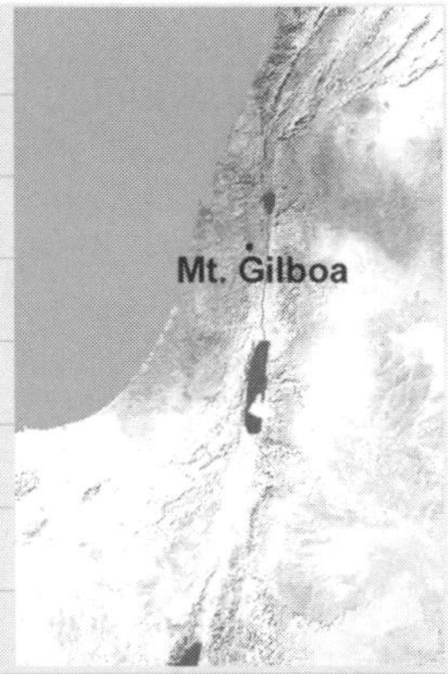

GILBOA (MOUNT)

Mount Gilboa is an extended ridge that rises on the southeastern side of the Jezreel Valley. The mountain marked the northernmost edge of the territory assigned to the tribe of Manasseh. Mount Gilboa offered strategic high ground to the Israelite army when facing foreign invaders in the Valley of Jezreel.

Period of the Judges *Judges 7*—Gideon chose his three hundred men at the spring of Harod that flows from the base of Mount Gilboa (called Mount Gilead in 7:3).

United Kingdom *1 Samuel 28:4–5; 31:1–5*—King Saul and his army camped on Mount Gilboa when they mobilized to fight the Philistines in the Jezreel Valley. The Philistines defeated Israel and killed Saul and his sons on Mount Gilboa.

2 Samuel 1:21—David lamented Saul's death and wished Mount Gilboa would become dry and barren because of the tragedy that had occurred on its slopes.

Looking down at the Jezreel Valley from Mount G

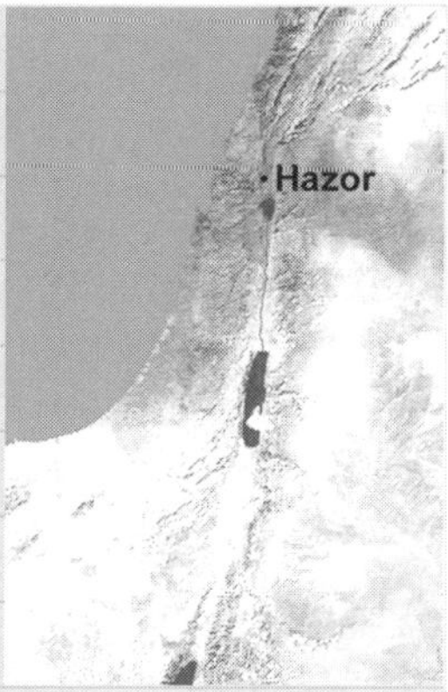

HAZOR

Hazor was to Israel in the Old Testament what Capernaum was to Israel in the New Testament. It was a strategic city because it was located on a well-defended hill that straddled the International Highway at a spot where it narrowed along the Jordan River. Thus, it served as a first line of defense against armies attacking from the north. It also guarded the trade routes and could be used to collect taxes and duties.

Period of Conquest *Joshua 11:1–13*—Joshua captured the city from Jabin, king of Hazor, and burned it. At this time it had a population of approximately 40,000 and was the largest city in the country.

Period of the Judges *Judges 4–5*—Hazor was rebuilt by another ruler named Jabin, who controlled the northern section of Israel for twenty years. This was the judgment of God on Israel for her sins: "The LORD sold them into the hands of Jabin, a king of Canaan, who reigned in Hazor" (Judg. 4:2). Under Deborah and Barak, Israel won a great victory over Sisera, Jabin's general, in the Jezreel Valley. For more information, see Megiddo.

United Kingdom *1 Kings 9:15*—Solomon rebuilt Hazor during his reign to guard the northern approach to the land of Israel.

Divided Kingdom *2 Kings 15:29*—The inhabitants of Hazor were taken into captivity by Tiglath-Pileser, king of Assyria.

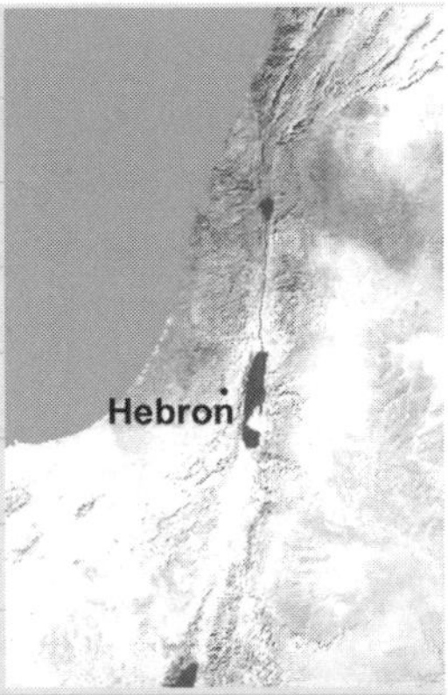

HEBRON/KIRIATH ARBA/MAMRE

Ancient Hebron served as the seedbed for the nation of Israel. Abraham dwelt in Hebron, and the only land he ever possessed was the burial cave he purchased here. Abraham, Sarah, Isaac, Rebekah, and Jacob were buried at the cave of Machpelah. Later, David ruled as king over Judah from Hebron. The remains of the shrine built over the cave of Machpelah by Herod the Great still stand in Hebron.

Patriarchal Period *Genesis 13:18*—Abram settled at "the great trees of Mamre at Hebron."

Genesis 14:11–16—Abram marched from Hebron to pursue the army of Kedorlaomer and rescue his nephew Lot.

Genesis 18:1–33—God's heavenly messengers paid a visit to Abraham at Hebron, and he haggled over the future of Sodom.

Genesis 19:27–29—Abraham viewed the destruction of Sodom from near Hebron.

Genesis 23:1–20—Sarah died in "Kiriath Arba (that is, Hebron)," and Abraham purchased the cave of Machpelah as a family burial plot.

Genesis 25:7–10—Abraham died and was buried with Sarah in the cave of Machpelah in Hebron.

Genesis 35:27–29—Isaac died and was buried in the cave of Machpelah in Hebron.

Genesis 49:29–33; 50:12–14—Jacob was buried in the cave of Machpelah in Hebron.

Period of Conquest *Joshua 10*—The king of Hebron joined the coalition that opposed Joshua and attacked Gibeon. Joshua attacked Hebron and killed its inhabitants (10:36–37).

Joshua 14:6–15; 15:13–14—Caleb personally requested the area surrounding Hebron as his tribal inheritance and drove out the remaining inhabitants.

Joshua 20:1–9—Hebron was named as one of the six cities of refuge in the land of Israel.

Joshua 21:11–12—The Levites were given Hebron as one of their forty-eight cities of inheritance throughout the land of Israel, but the fields and surrounding villages belonged to Caleb and his descendants.

Period of the Judges *Judges 16:1–3*—Samson carried the city gates of Gaza to Hebron.

United Kingdom *1 Samuel 30:26–31*—David sent some of the spoils of war to Hebron and other cities he had visited as a fugitive from Saul.

2 Samuel 2:1–4, 11—David was anointed king over Judah at Hebron.

2 Samuel 15:1–12—Absalom conspired against his father, David, to take over the kingdom and went to Hebron to be proclaimed king.

Divided Kingdom *2 Chronicles 11:10*—King Rehoboam of Judah fortified Hebron for the defense of his kingdom.

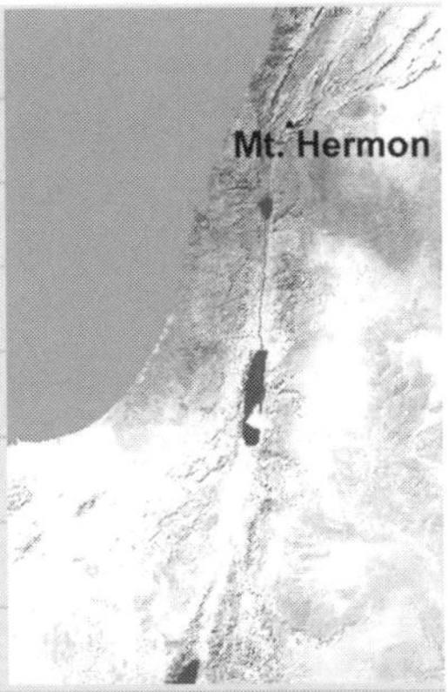

HERMON (MOUNT)

Mount Hermon, on the northeastern fringe of ancient Israel, rises majestically to a height of over 9,000 feet. The mountain stood as a symbol of beauty, fertility, and abundance. Some believe this is the Mount of Transfiguration.

Period of the Exodus *Deuteronomy 3:8–11*—Israel defeated Og, king of Bashan, whose kingdom stretched "as far as Mount Hermon."

Period of Conquest *Joshua 11:3, 17; 12:1, 5; 13:5, 11*—Mount Hermon marked the northern limits of Joshua's conquests.

United Kingdom *Psalm 133:3; Song of Songs 4:8*—Mount Hermon was used in poetry by David and Solomon. Its height and beauty symbolized a place of joy and fruitfulness.

Divided Kingdom *Psalms 42:6; 89:12*—Psalmists saw Mount Hermon picturing God's majesty or standing as the silent sentinel on the edge of God's Promised Land.

Life of Christ *Matthew 17:1–9; Mark 9:2–9; Luke 9:28–37*—Mount Hermon is considered by some to be the "Mount of Transfiguration" because of its height. (Matthew 17:1 and Mark 9:2 speak of a "high mountain," and Mount Hermon rises over 9,000 feet while Mount Tabor is only 1,850 feet high.)

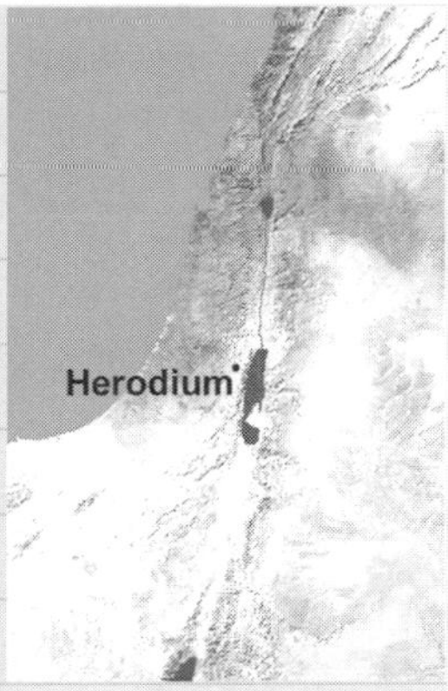

HERODIUM

Within viewing distance of Bethlehem stands the Herodium, one of Herod the Great's palaces/fortresses that became his place of burial. It is ironic that the "king by might" was buried just a short distance from the birthplace of the "King by Right," whom Herod had tried so hard to destroy. From the Herodium, one can see the towers on the Mount of Olives to the northwest, the village of Bethlehem to the west, and the Judean Wilderness and Dead Sea to the east. This is the wilderness in which David shepherded his flocks as a boy (cf. Psalm 23).

The famous silhouette of the Herodium against the Israeli sky

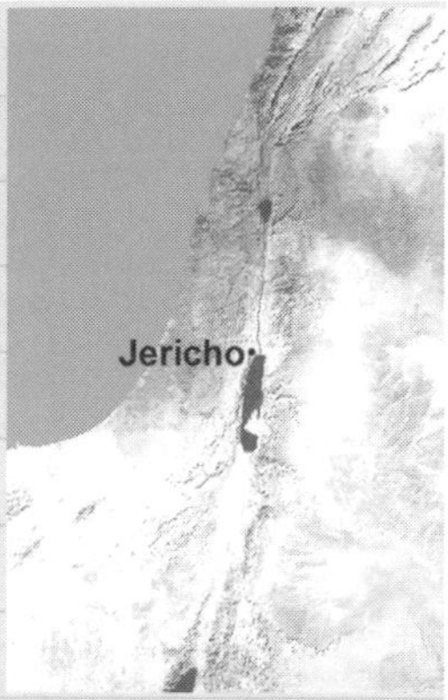

JERICHO

Archaeological excavations have shown that civilization existed in Jericho from very ancient times. It is one of the world's oldest cities. The site became so important because of its warm climate, abundant springs of water, and strategic location astride a point where caravans could travel east to west along the Jordan Valley.

Period of Conquest *Joshua 2*—Rahab received and hid the spies in Jericho.

Round Neolithic tower at Old Testa Jericho, one of the oldest structures built

Joshua 6—Joshua captured Jericho by marching around it seven days. Rahab and her family were spared.

Period of the Judges *Judges 3:12–30*—Eglon, king of Moab, oppressed Israel and ruled from Jericho, which was called "the City of Palms" (Judg. 3:13). He was defeated by Ehud.

United Kingdom *2 Samuel 10:4–5*—After David's envoy to the Ammonites had been publicly humiliated, they waited at Jericho until their beards had grown back.

Divided Kingdom *1 Kings 16:34*—Jericho was rebuilt as a city in the time of Ahab, king of Israel. The builder sacrificed two of his sons to the false gods in an attempt to guarantee their favor in his task, thus fulfilling Joshua's prediction (Josh. 6:26).

2 Kings 2:4–22—Elijah and Elisha ministered in Jericho, and both crossed the Jordan River on dry ground nearby. The bitter water was made pure by Elisha at Jericho.

Babylonian Captivity *2 Kings 25:4–6; Jeremiah 39:4–6*—After Jerusalem's fall to the Babylonians in 586 BC, King Zedekiah fled from Jerusalem through the Judean Wilderness toward the Jordan Valley. He was captured by the Babylonians on the "plains of Jericho."

Restoration *Ezra 2:34; Nehemiah 3:2; 7:36*—During the return from Babylon, 345 men from Jericho made the journey back to their hometown. They also helped rebuild the walls of Jerusalem.

Life of Christ Herod the Great built his palace and administrative buildings approximately one mile south of the mound on which Old Testament Jericho had been built. The "new" city of Jericho served as one of Herod the Great's winter palaces.

Matthew 4:1–11; Mark 1:12–13; Luke 4:1–13—Jesus was tempted by Satan in the Judean Wilderness. The traditional site of this temptation is the nearby Mount of Temptation.

Luke 19:1–10—Zacchaeus was converted in Jericho after Jesus spotted him in a sycamore fig tree.

Matthew 20:29–34; Mark 10:46–52; Luke 18:35–43—Christ healed blind Bartimaeus and his companion in Jericho during His final trip to Jerusalem.

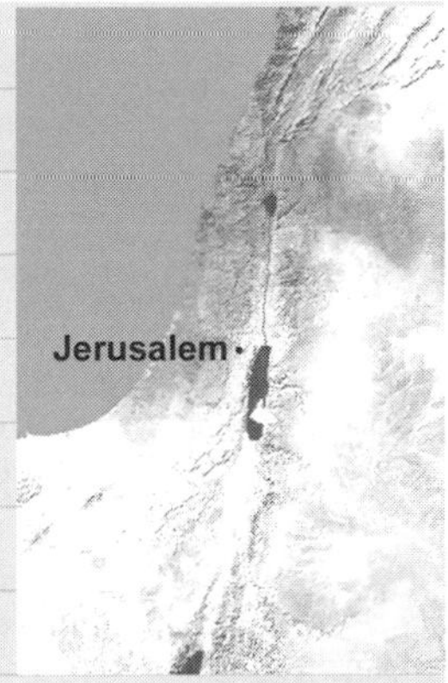

JERUSALEM

Jerusalem, the capital of ancient Israel, stands as one of the most important cities in all the world. But its importance comes ultimately from God. It is "the city the LORD had chosen . . . in which to put his Name" (1 Kings 14:21; see also 2 Chron. 6:6). From its selection as "the City of David" to the eternal glory of the "new Jerusalem," this city occupies a primary place in God's work on earth.

The Western (Wailing) Wall, Judaism's holiest site, with the Dome of the Rock in the background

Patriarchal Period *Genesis 14:17–24*—Abram paid tithes to Melchizedek (whose name means "my king is righteousness") in the city of Salem.

Genesis 22—Abraham prepared to offer Isaac on Mount Moriah, the mountain on the northern edge of ancient Jerusalem, which is now covered by the Dome of the Rock.

Period of Conquest *Joshua 10:1–11*—Joshua defeated Adoni-Zedek, king of Jerusalem.

Judges 1:1, 8—The tribe of Judah captured Jerusalem and killed its inhabitants, but apparently they did not occupy the city that was soon reoccupied by the Jebusites (Judg. 1:21).

Period of the Judges *Judges 19:10–11*—Jerusalem was known as "Jebus" and the "city of the Jebusites."

United Kingdom *2 Samuel 5:5–16*—David captured, strengthened, and beautified the city, making it his capital. (David reigned seven-and-a-half years in Hebron and thirty-three years in Jerusalem, 1010–970 BC.) David called Jerusalem "the City of David" (2 Sam. 5:9). The city at that time occupied only the cone-shaped spur of land south of the Temple Mount that is outside the present-day city walls.

2 Samuel 6:1–12—David brought the ark of the covenant to Jerusalem.

2 Samuel 24:18–25; 2 Chronicles 3:1—David purchased the threshing floor of Araunah the Jebusite, which later became the site of Solomon's temple.

1 Kings 2:10—David was buried in Jerusalem.

1 Kings 6–9—Solomon, who reigned from 970–931 BC, built the temple and other magnificent buildings. He expanded the city of Jerusalem north so that it included the original City of David and Mount Moriah.

Divided Kingdom *1 Kings 14:25–28*—Shishak, king of Egypt, attacked and plundered Jerusalem in 926 BC during the reign of Rehoboam, son of Solomon.

2 Chronicles 21:16–17—The Philistines and Arabs attacked and plundered Jerusalem about 845 BC during the reign of Jehoram. This attack could be the basis for Obadiah's prophecy.

2 Chronicles 25:17–24—The northern kingdom of Israel attacked and plundered Jerusalem (and tore down a section of its walls) about 785 BC during the reign of Amaziah.

Single Kingdom *2 Kings 18; 2 Chronicles 32:30; Isaiah 36–37*—Sennacherib, king of Assyria, surrounded Jerusalem in 701 BC. King Hezekiah went to Isaiah to ask for the Lord's deliverance, and God killed 185,000 Assyrian troops, sparing Jerusalem from attack. Sometime just prior to this invasion, Hezekiah had expanded the city of Jerusalem to include the Western Hill (today mistakenly called "Mount Zion"). The city had greatly expanded in size because of the influx of refugees following the fall of the northern kingdom of Israel to Assyria in 721 BC.

Babylonian Captivity *2 Kings 25:1–6; Jeremiah 39:1–6*—After a thirty-month siege, Nebuchadnezzar of Babylon captured, sacked, and burned Jerusalem in 586 BC.

King Zedekiah fled Jerusalem, but the Babylonians captured him on the plains of Jericho.

Restoration *Ezra 1–6*—Under Zerubbabel, almost fifty thousand Jews returned from Babylon in 537 BC and laid the foundation of the temple in 536. After a sixteen-year delay, they resumed work on the temple in 520 BC and completed it in 516. Ezra journeyed to Jerusalem in 457 BC.

Nehemiah 1–6—Nehemiah rebuilt the walls of Jerusalem about 444 BC. Some parts of his walls can still be seen along the eastern ridge of the original City of David.

Intertestamental Era Alexander the Great captured Jerusalem in 332 BC. Josephus recorded that the city was spared when the high priest showed Alexander the prophecies of Daniel, which predicted Alexander's defeat of the Persians (*Antiquities* 11.8.5).

Herod the Great built his temple in Jerusalem, starting in 20 BC.

Life of Christ *Luke 2:22, 27, 41–52*—Jesus was presented at the temple as an infant and visited the temple at age twelve.

Luke 19:45–48; John 2:12–25—Twice, at the opening and the closing of His ministry, Jesus cleansed the temple.

John 5:7–9—Jesus healed a man at the Pool of Bethesda in Jerusalem.

Matthew 21:1–11; Mark 11:1–11; Luke 19:28–44; John 12:12–19—Jesus rode down the Mount of Olives to Jerusalem and made His formal presentation to Israel as the Messiah.

Matthew 24–25—On the Mount of Olives, Jesus delivered the Olivet Discourse and foretold the destruction of the temple.

John 13–16—In an upper room Jesus washed the disciples' feet, instituted the Lord's Supper, and delivered the Upper Room Discourse.

Matthew 27–28; Mark 15–16; Luke 23–24; John 19–20—Jesus was tried, crucified, buried, and resurrected in Jerusalem. His final ascension to heaven took place east of Jerusalem on the Mount of Olives.

Apostolic Age *Acts 2*—The Holy Spirit descended on the disciples who were gathered in Jerusalem on the day of Pentecost, and the church was born.

Acts 3:2, 11; 5:21—Peter and the other apostles preached at the temple.

Acts 7—Stephen was martyred in Jerusalem.

Acts 9—Saul left Jerusalem for Damascus and was converted.

Acts 15—The first church council convened in Jerusalem.

Acts 21:17–23; 23—Paul, after his third missionary journey, visited Jerusalem, where he was seized by the Jews during a visit to the temple.

Post-Apostolic History of Jerusalem

Roman Era (63 BC–AD 330). The Roman general Titus destroyed Jerusalem in AD 70. It was destroyed again by Emperor Hadrian in AD 135 following the Bar Kochba revolt. Hadrian rebuilt the city and renamed it Aelia Capitolina. The street called the Cardo (and the overall layout of Jerusalem today) dates to this period.

Post-Roman Eras are: Byzantine Era, 330–634; Arab Era, 634–1099; Crusader Period, 1099–1187 and 1229–1244; Arab

Era, 1187–1517, except 1229–1244; Turkish Era, 1517–1917; British Era,1917–1948; Jordanian Era, 1948–1967; Israeli Independence, 1967. The present city walls were built by Suleiman I during the Turkish Era.

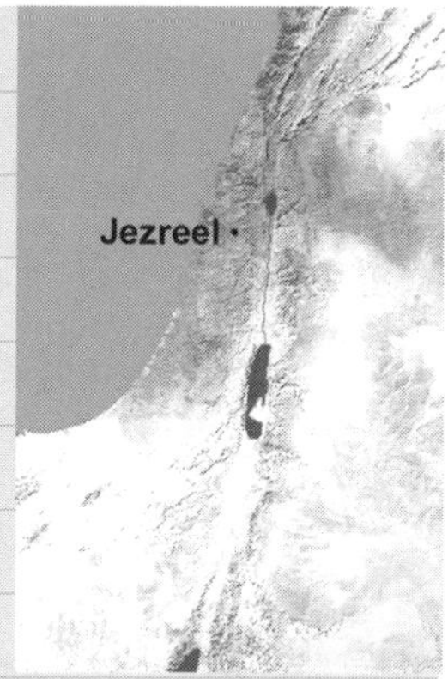

JEZREEL

The city of Jezreel sits on the northwestern edge of Mount Gilboa overlooking the Jezreel Valley. The valley likely took its name from the city.

Period of Conquest *Joshua 19:18*—God allotted the city of Jezreel to the tribe of Issachar.

Divided Kingdom *1 Kings 18:45–46*—Elijah outran Ahab's chariot from Mount Carmel to Jezreel.

1 Kings 21:1–24—Ahab and Jezebel coveted and seized the vineyard of Naboth in Jezreel. Elijah condemned their murder of Naboth and predicted God's destruction of their royal line.

2 Kings 8:28–29; 9:14–37—The kings of Israel and Judah returned from battle to rest and recuperate at Jezreel. Jehu rode up the valley from the Jordan River and killed both kings as well as Queen Jezebel.

2 Kings 10:1–11; Hosea 1:4—Jehu massacred all Ahab's descendants at Jezreel. The prophet Hosea condemned this bloodshed.

JEZREEL (VALLEY OF)

The arrowhead-shaped Valley of Jezreel, twenty miles long and fourteen miles wide at its broadest point, is an apt stage for the historical dramas played out on its floor. The valley served as a crossroads, with the International Highway from Egypt to Mesopotamia intersecting a major east–west road from the Mediterranean Sea to the Jordan Valley and beyond. To understand the importance of the valley, look up the cities and mountains that ring this stage. Those included in this book are Beth Shan, Mount Carmel, Mount Gilboa, the city of Jezreel, Megiddo, the Hill of Moreh, Nazareth, and Mount Tabor.

The spring of Harod, where Gideon chose his 300 men, flows from the base of Mount Gilboa into the Jezreel Valley.

Period of Conquest *Joshua 17:16*—God allotted the Valley of Jezreel to the tribe of Manasseh, but they could not take it because the inhabitants of the valley used "iron chariots."

Period of the Judges *Judges 6:33–37; 7:1–25*—Gideon defeated the Midianites in the Valley of Jezreel. Gideon and his men camped on Mount Gilboa while the Midianites camped on the Hill of Moreh.

United Kingdom *1 Samuel 29:1; 31:1–8*—Saul was killed by the Philistines on Mount Gilboa at the southeastern end of the Valley of Jezreel.

1 Kings 4:12—Solomon placed Beth Shan, Megiddo, and Jezreel under the governorship of Baana, son of Ahilud.

Divided Kingdom *1 Kings 18:45–19:2*—Ahab and Jezebel had a residence in the city of Jezreel, which is in the Valley of Jezreel. After the contest with the prophets of Baal on Mount Carmel, Elijah outran Ahab's chariot to Jezreel, where Jezebel threatened to have him killed.

2 Kings 4:8–37—The prophet Elisha raised the Shunammite woman's son back to life. (Shunem is located in the Jezreel Valley on the southern slope of the Hill of Moreh.)

2 Kings 9:14–37—Jehu killed Joram, king of Israel (Ahab's son); Ahaziah, king of Judah; and Jezebel in Jezreel.

Hosea 1:4–5—The prophet Hosea named his first child "Jezreel" as a sign to show Israel that God would allow Israel to be defeated in the Jezreel Valley for the bloodshed of Jehu and his successors at the city of Jezreel.

Life of Christ *Luke 7:11–17*—Jesus visited the town of Nain on the northern slope of the Hill of Moreh and raised a woman's young son to life.

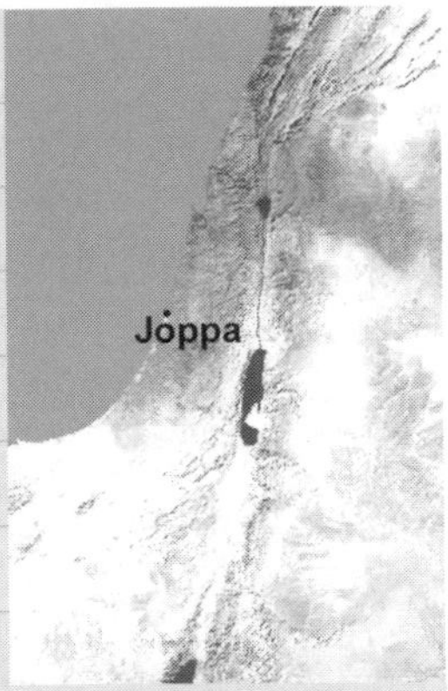

JOPPA/JAFFA/TEL AVIV

The port city of Joppa (modern Jaffa) served as Israel's link to the sea throughout the Old Testament. Today, the city of Tel Aviv sits on the north side of Jaffa and dwarfs Israel's ancient seaport.

Period of Conquest *Joshua 19:46–47*—God allotted the city of Joppa to the tribe of Dan, but they failed to capture it.

United Kingdom *2 Chronicles 2:16*—During Solomon's reign, Joppa served as the chief seaport of Jerusalem. Cedars from Lebanon were floated down to Joppa and then transported to Jerusalem for the building of the temple.

Divided Kingdom *Jonah 1:3*—Jonah sailed from Joppa when he tried to flee to Tarshish rather than obey God's command to go to Nineveh.

Restoration *Ezra 3:7*—Cedars from Lebanon were again floated down to Joppa for the rebuilding of the temple.

Apostolic Age *Acts 9:36–43*—Peter raised Dorcas to life at Joppa.

Acts 10—Peter had a vision on the housetop of Simon the tanner in Joppa showing him God wanted him to share His "good news" with the Gentiles. This led to Peter's ministry in the house of Cornelius at Caesarea.

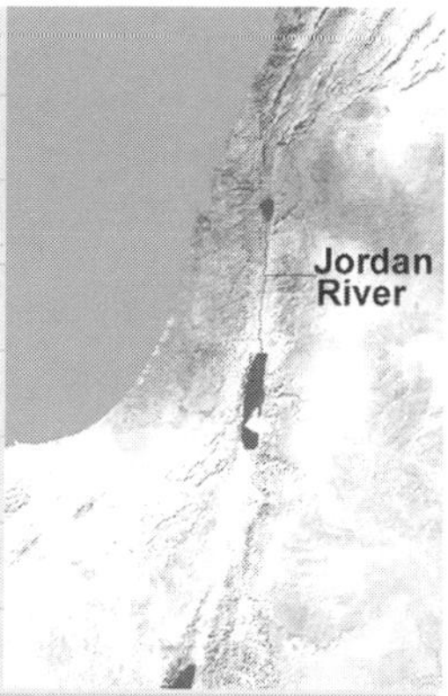

JORDAN RIVER

The Jordan River (meaning "go down") flows from the Sea of Galilee to the Dead Sea. Although the actual distance between these two bodies of water is less than 70 miles, the Jordan River snakes along in a winding path that gives the river a final length of almost 110 miles. There were some settlements along the river (notably Beth Shan in the north and Jericho in the south), but the area was not generally favorable for settlement. Instead, much of the area along the Jordan River was covered with dense vegetation that hid wild animals (see Jer. 12:5; 49:19; 50:44). Today the Jordan River is not impressive. It is actually a small stream less than fifty feet wide most of the year. Much of the water that once fed the Jordan River is now used for irrigation.

The waters of the Jordan River as it meanders through Israel

Patriarchal Period *Genesis 13:10–11*—Lot chose the "plain of the Jordan" near Jericho when he and his family separated from Abram. Lot selected the area because it was "well watered . . . like the land of Egypt." Lot later moved to Sodom and Gomorrah at the southern end of the Dead Sea.

Period of the Exodus *Numbers 34:10–12*—God identified the Jordan River as the eastern border of Israel.

Period of Conquest *Numbers 22:1*—Just before entering the Promised Land, the Israelites camped on the plains of Moab by the Jordan River.

Joshua 3:1–4:18—Joshua led Israel across the Jordan River while God stopped the waters upstream at the town of Adam.

Period of the Judges *Judges 3:28–30*—Ehud and the Israelites seized control of the "fords of the Jordan" to cut off Moab's escape. Controlling this strategic crossing point allowed them to destroy Moab's occupying army.

Judges 7:24–25—Gideon and the Israelites seized control of the "waters of the Jordan" to prohibit the Midianites from escaping across the river.

Judges 12:1–7—Jephthah and the Israelites of Gilead fought against the tribe of Ephraim. In the battle, Jephthah's men seized the "fords of the Jordan" and killed the soldiers of Ephraim who tried to escape.

United Kingdom *1 Samuel 31:7–10*—Following the Philistines' defeat of Saul, the Israelites along the northern Jordan Valley fled. The Philistines occupied the land, including the city of Beth Shan.

2 Samuel 17:15–22—When Absalom rebelled against his father, King David fled across the Jordan River to escape his son's army.

2 Chronicles 4:16–17—The large bronze objects for Solomon's temple were cast in clay molds "in the plain of the Jordan."

Divided Kingdom *2 Kings 2:7–14*—Elijah and Elisha crossed the Jordan on dry ground. After Elijah's translation into heaven, Elisha repeated the miracle on his return into the land of Israel.

2 Kings 5:9–15—The Syrian general Naaman was healed of leprosy after obeying Elisha's orders and dipping himself seven times in the Jordan River.

2 Kings 6:3–7—Elisha caused an ax head to float after it had fallen into the Jordan River.

Psalm 114:3–5—The psalmist remembered God's great miracle in turning back the waters of the Jordan River.

Micah 6:5—Micah reminded the Israelites of their journey "from Shittim to Gilgal," a reference to their journey through the Jordan River on dry ground.

Single Kingdom *Jeremiah 12:5*—God rebuked Jeremiah by warning him that if he was having trouble now in the "safe country," the going would become more difficult in the "thickets by the Jordan."

Babylonian Captivity *Ezekiel 47:18*—God identified the Jordan River as the future eastern border of Israel.

Restoration *Zechariah 11:3*—Lions lived in the thick vegetation along the Jordan River.

Life of Christ *Matthew 3:5–6; Mark 1:5; John 1:28*—John the Baptist baptized in the Jordan River.

Matthew 3:13–17; Mark 1:9—Jesus was baptized in the Jordan River.

John 10:40–42—Jesus "went back across the Jordan" to the location where John the Baptist had first been baptizing.

JUDEAN WILDERNESS

The Judean Wilderness extends from just north of Jerusalem to the southern tip of the Dead Sea. The strip of land itself is ten to twenty miles wide and lies between the hill country of Judah and the Rift Valley. This land is in the "rain shadow"—that area on the east side of the hill country that receives little rain from the Mediterranean Sea. The area experiences a tremendous drop in elevation. From Jerusalem to Jericho (a distance of approximately thirteen miles), the land drops from 2,600 feet above sea level to 1,100 feet below sea level—a drop of 3,700 feet! In the Old Testament, individual portions of the Judean Wilderness were often named for nearby towns and villages (the Desert of En Gedi, the Desert of Maon, the Desert of Tekoa, and the Desert of Ziph).

The Judean Wilderness with springtime flowers

Period of Conquest *Joshua 7:24–26*—The Israelites stoned to death Achan and his family in the "Valley of Achor" for his sin at Jericho.

Joshua 10:7–9—Joshua and the Israelites marched through the Judean Wilderness at night as they went from Gilgal to Gibeon to rescue the Gibeonites.

Joshua 15:61–63—Part of the tribal allotment for Judah included the land "in the desert"—a reference to the Judean Wilderness.

Period of the Judges *Judges 20:47*—After the intertribal warfare in Israel, only the six hundred Benjamites who fled "into the desert to the rock of Rimmon" remained alive.

United Kingdom *1 Samuel 23:15–29*—David hid from Saul in the "Desert of Ziph."

1 Samuel 24:1–22—David spared Saul's life in the "Desert of En Gedi."

1 Samuel 25:1–40—In the "Desert of Maon," Nabal refused to help David and was struck dead. David took Abigail to be his wife.

1 Samuel 26:1–25—In the "Desert of Ziph," David again spared Saul's life.

2 Samuel 16:5–14—Shimei cursed David as he traveled east from Jerusalem through the Judean Wilderness to flee Absalom.

Song of Songs 3:6–11—The daughters of Jerusalem were summoned to watch Solomon "coming up from the desert" to Jerusalem for his wedding.

Divided Kingdom *2 Chronicles 20:1–24*—King Jehoshaphat led his people into the "Desert of Tekoa" to repel a threatened attack against Jerusalem. The invaders were coming from En Gedi.

Isaiah 40:1–11—The prophet Isaiah looked forward to a time when a voice crying in the wilderness would announce a message of comfort to Jerusalem.

Hosea 2:14–15—Hosea predicted a time when God would bring the nation of Israel "into the desert" in a second exodus. This time God would make "the Valley of Achor a door of hope."

Single Kingdom *Jeremiah 17:5–8*—Jeremiah announced that those who put their trust in people rather than God would be like "a bush in the wastelands" that would dwell in the "parched places of the desert."

Babylonian Captivity *2 Kings 25:4–6; Jeremiah 39:4–6*—After Jerusalem's fall to the Babylonians in 586 BC, King Zedekiah fled from Jerusalem through the Judean Wilderness toward the Jordan Valley. He was captured by the Babylonians on the plains of Jericho.

Ezekiel 47:8–12—Ezekiel described a time when a permanent stream of living water would flow from Jerusalem toward "the eastern region" to bring life to a barren land.

Life of Christ *Matthew 3:1–3; Mark 1:4–5; Luke 3:2*—John the Baptist began his ministry in the "Desert of Judea."

Matthew 4:1–11; Mark 1:12–13; Luke 4:1–13—After His baptism in the Jordan, Jesus was led into the desert to be tempted for forty days.

Luke 10:25–37—Jesus' parable of the good Samaritan was set in the Judean Wilderness between Jerusalem and Jericho.

John 11:54—After raising Lazarus from the dead, Jesus withdrew with His disciples "to a region near the desert, to a village called Ephraim."

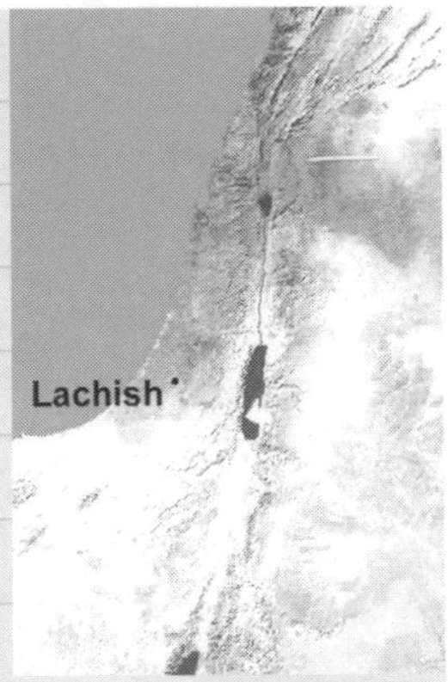

LACHISH

The city of Lachish guarded a major road through Judah's foothills from the coast to the city of Hebron. The city's location and strong natural defenses gave it strategic importance. Ultimately, the city of Lachish became second in importance only to Jerusalem during the latter part of the kingdom of Judah.

Period of Conquest *Joshua 10*—The king of Lachish joined the coalition that opposed Joshua and attacked Gibeon. Joshua attacked Lachish and killed its inhabitants.

Joshua 15:39—God allotted Lachish to the tribe of Judah.

The gate complex of ancient Lachish, Judah's domi
city in the low hills of the Sheph

Divided Kingdom *2 Chronicles 11:9*—King Rehoboam of Judah fortified Lachish for the defense of his kingdom.

2 Kings 14:17–20; 2 Chronicles 25:27–28—King Amaziah fled from Jerusalem to Lachish to avoid an assassination attempt, but the conspirators went to Lachish and killed him there.

Single Kingdom *2 Kings 18:14, 17; 19:8; 2 Chronicles 32:9; Isaiah 36:2; 37:8; Micah 1:13*—Sennacherib, king of Assyria, invaded Judah and sent his army against Lachish. The city fell to Sennacherib in 701 BC. He commemorated the victory with a series of reliefs carved on his palace walls in Nineveh depicting the siege and capture of Lachish.

Jeremiah 34:7—Nebuchadnezzar, king of Babylon, invaded Judah and sent his army against Judah's cities. Near the end of his invasion, only Lachish, Azekah, and Jerusalem remained unconquered. Eventually, all three cities fell.

Restoration *Nehemiah 11:30*—Some of the remnant who returned from the Babylonian captivity reinhabited Lachish.

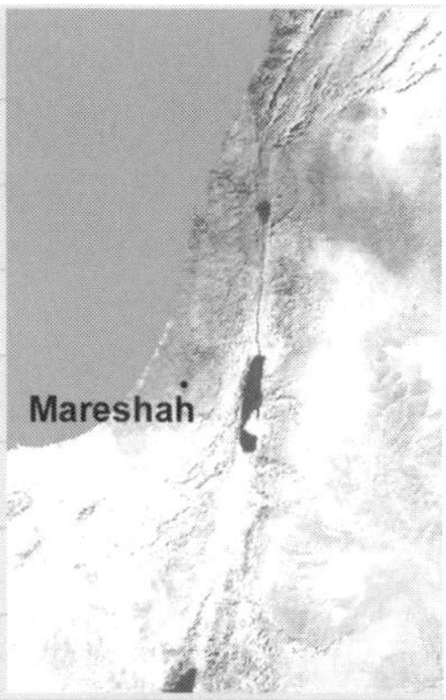

MARESHAH/GUVRIN

The Guvrin Valley itself is one of the five major valleys running east–west through the foothills between the coastal plain and the hill country of Judah. While it did not occupy a place of great importance during the biblical periods, two cities named by the prophet Micah, Mareshah and Moresheth-gath (Micah's hometown), are in this area.

During the time of Judah's exile in Babylon, the Edomites gained control of the land, and the city of Mareshah became part of their kingdom. In 113 BC John Hyrcanus captured and destroyed Mareshah and forced the Edomites to convert to Judaism or to leave the land.

Sidonian tomb in Mare

The area remained under strong Jewish influence until the time of the second Jewish revolt against Rome in AD 132–135, often called the Bar Kochba revolt. At that time the Romans destroyed the Jewish settlements in the area. A new city eventually sprang up called Eleuthropolis ("free city") that became one of the largest cities in the land during the Roman and Byzantine periods.

Period of the Conquest *Joshua 15:44*—Mareshah was allotted to the tribe of Judah and was inhabited by the descendants of Caleb.

Divided Kingdom *2 Chronicles 11:8*—King Rehoboam of Judah fortified Mareshah for the defense of his kingdom.

2 Chronicles 14:9–12—King Asa of Judah defeated Zerah the Cushite in a battle that took place at Mareshah.

2 Chronicles 20:37—The prophet Eliezer from Mareshah announced God's displeasure with King Jehoshaphat of Judah for his alliance with King Ahaziah of Israel.

Micah 1:1, 14–15—Micah the prophet announced the destruction of the cities of Moresheth-gath and Mareshah.

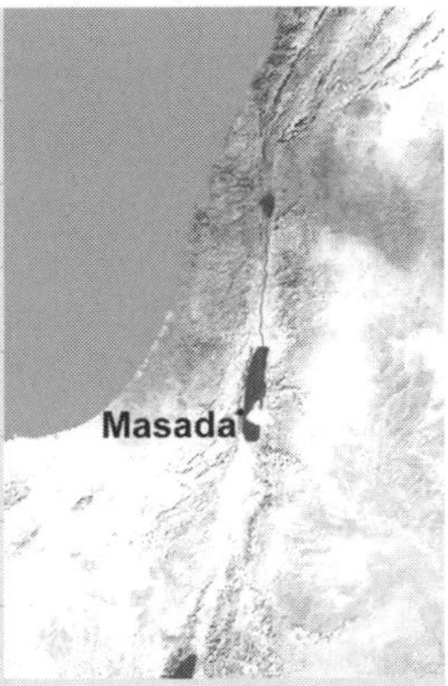

MASADA

Masada, a natural mesa near the western shore of the Dead Sea, matches well its Hebrew name, "the stronghold" (Hebrew *metsuda*). Masada is a shrine and symbol of modern Israel.

United Kingdom *1 Samuel 22:3–5; 1 Chronicles 12:1–16*—After taking his parents to Moab for safety, David and his four hundred men returned to Judah and temporarily camped "in the stronghold." Some Old Testament scholars identify this location with Masada.

1 Samuel 24:22—After confronting Saul at En Gedi, David fled to the "stronghold."

Intertestamental Era Herod the Great (37–4 BC) fortified Masada ("stronghold" or "fortress"), surrounding the top with a wall eighteen feet high. He also built a winter palace here, and the site was considered impregnable.

Apostolic Age When Jerusalem fell to the Romans in AD 70, Jewish patriots, under the leadership of Eliezer Ben Yair, fled to Masada, where they took their final stand against Rome. Finally, on April 15, AD 73, the Romans broke into the fortress and found that all of the defenders except two women and five children had killed each other. According to the Jewish historian Josephus, 960 people took their own lives at Masada, choosing death over slavery to Rome.

The Holy Land

I S R A E L

Looking down
the Jezreel Val
from the Mou
Precipice, the
from which th
people of Naz
sought to thro
Jesus (Luke 4:2

Canaanite "high place" at Megiddo.

The hill of Golgotha, or Place of the Skull, one of the traditional sites of Jesus' crucifixion.

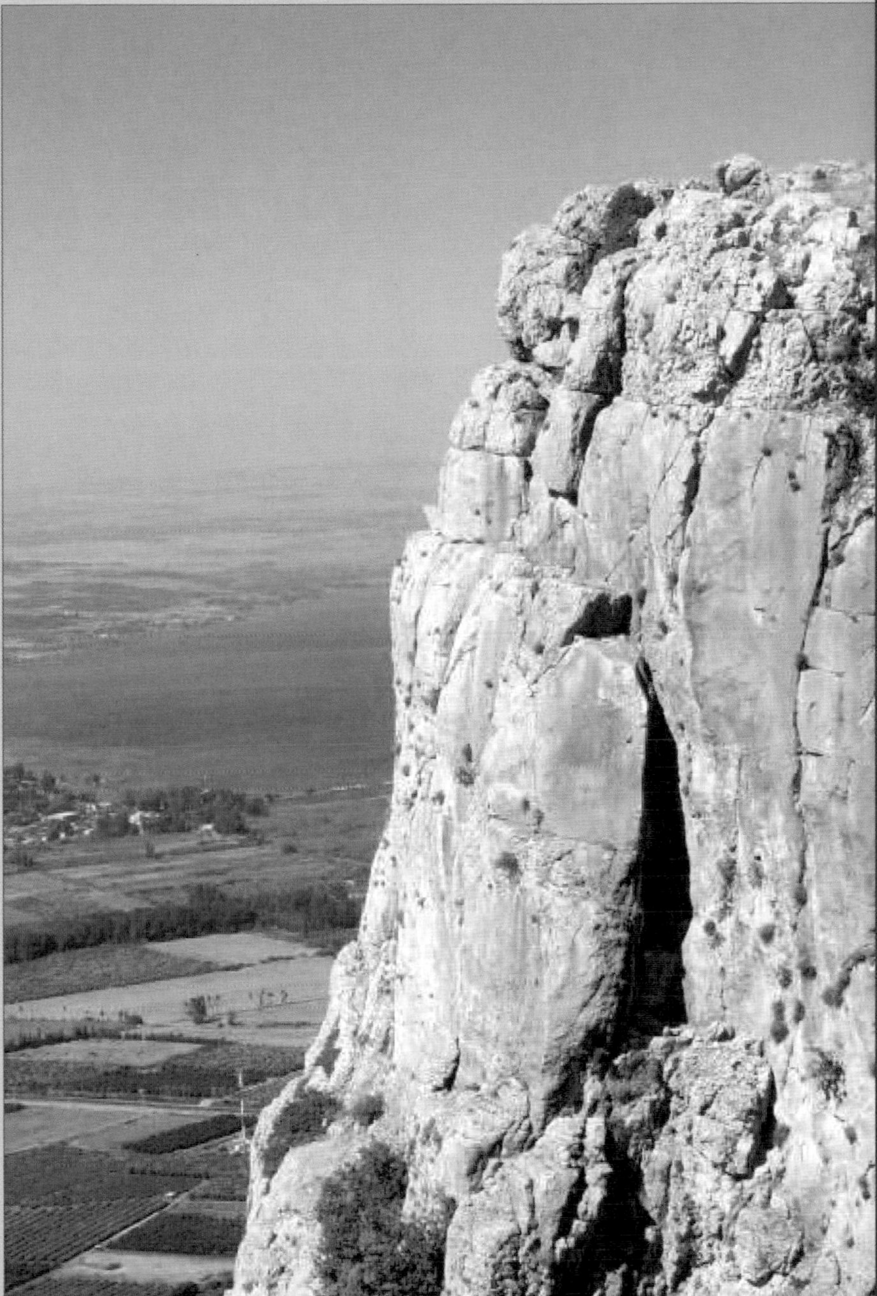

Cliffs of Mount Arbel with the Sea of Galilee in the background.

An ancient tomb near the side of the road illustrates what Joseph of Arimathea's tomb might have looked like from the outside.

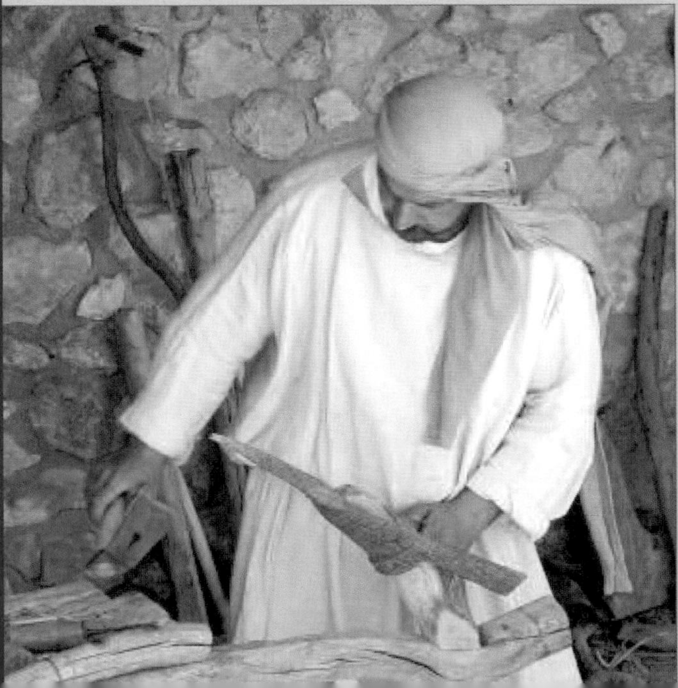

Carpenter in Nazareth repairing his plow.

The Mount of Temptation as seen from Jericho.

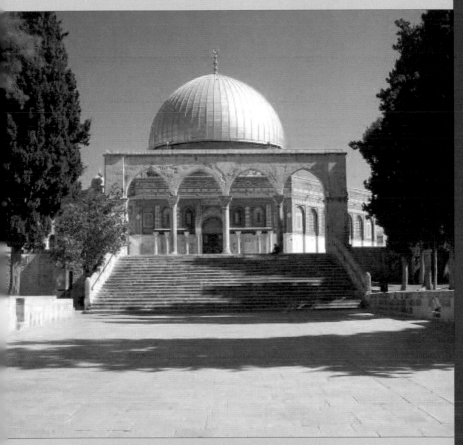

A closeup view of the Dome of the Rock built on the site of Solomon's temple.

Fisherman preparing to cast his net on the Sea of Galilee.

Walking through Hezekiah's tunnel from the Gihon spring to the Pool of Siloam.

Two ibex walking through the nature reserve at En Gedi.

Model of Herod's temple showing view into the inner court.

EGYPT

Sunrise from the summit of Mount Sinai.

Avenue of sphinxes at the entrance to the temple of Karnak.

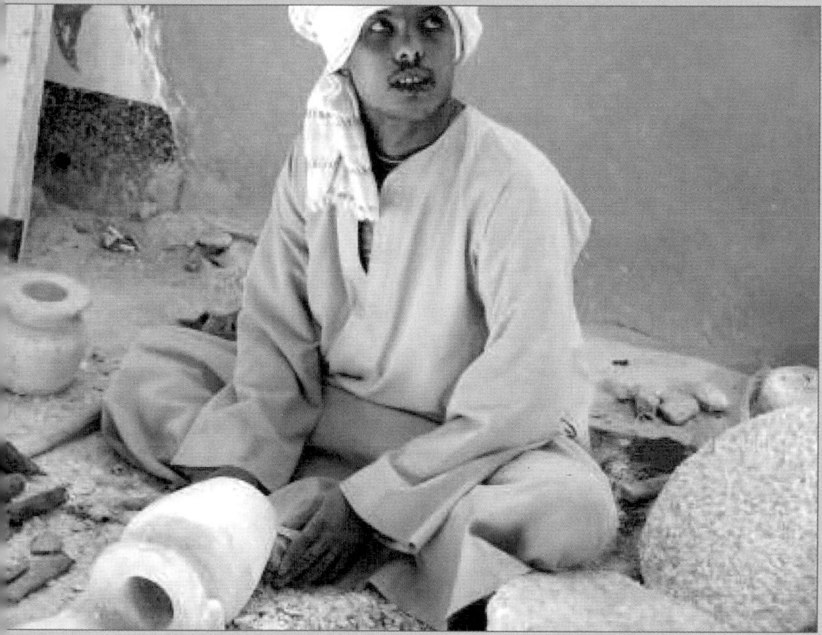

Craftsman carving an alabaster jar near the Valley of the Kings across from Karnak.

The Alabaster Sphinx in ancient Memphis, which some believe was carved in the likeness of Queen Hatshepsut who once ruled as pharaoh.

GREECE

Inscription at Corinth that names Erastus, most likely the city treasurer identified by Paul in Romans 16:23.

Looking up at the Acropolis in Athens from the Areopagus (Mars Hil

J O R D A N

The cardo (main north/south street) in the ancient city of Gerasa, today called Jerash.

The altar carved into the rock at the high place of Petra.

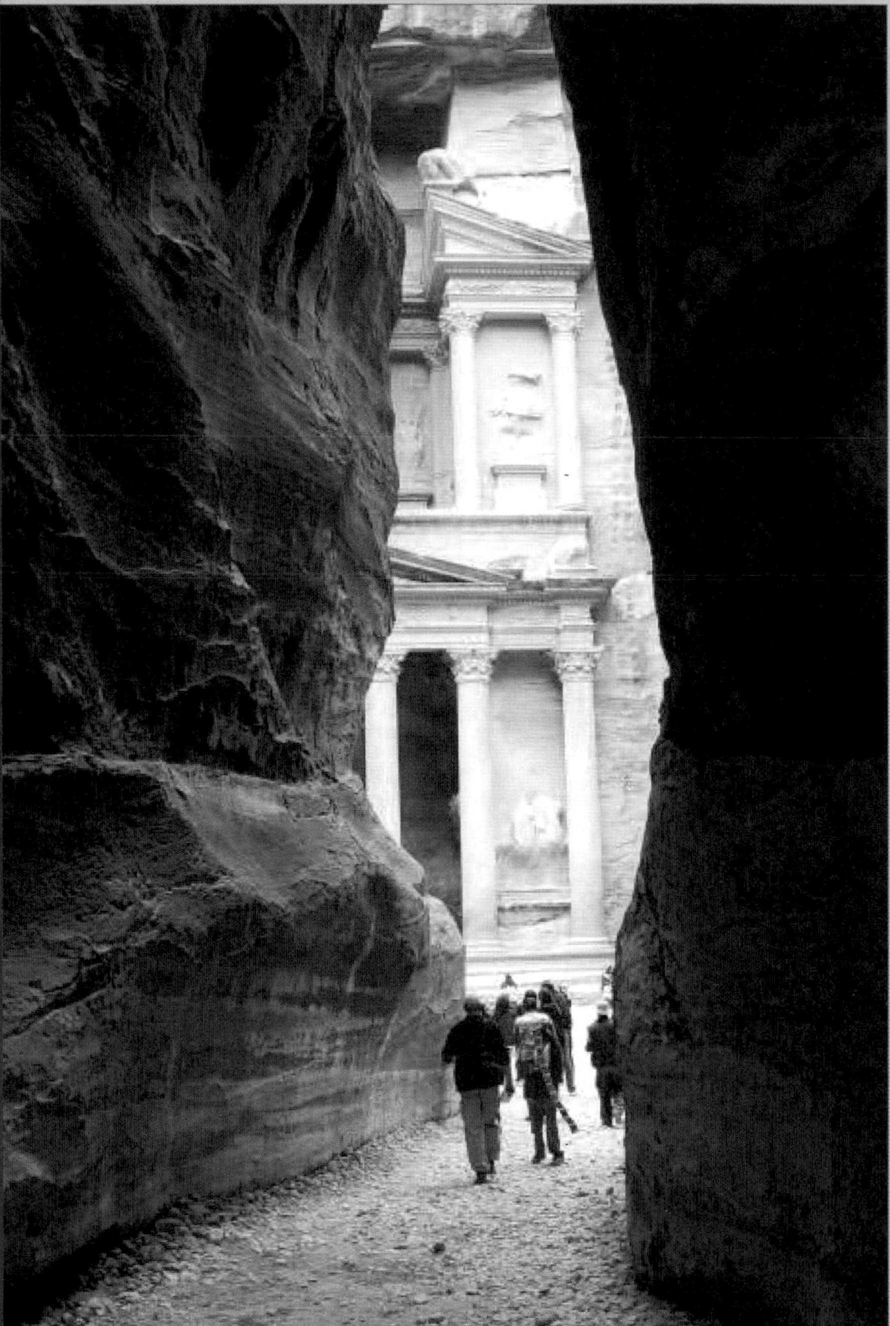

Walking through the Siq into Petra.

View west toward the Dead Sea from Machaerus, Jordan.

TURKEY

A partially excavated street in the ruins of ancient Laodicea.

The stadium in the ancient city of Aphrodisias in Turkey helps visualize the command in Hebrews 12:1 to "run with endurance the race that is set before us."

The re-erected marble façade of the Library of Celsus at ancient Ephesus

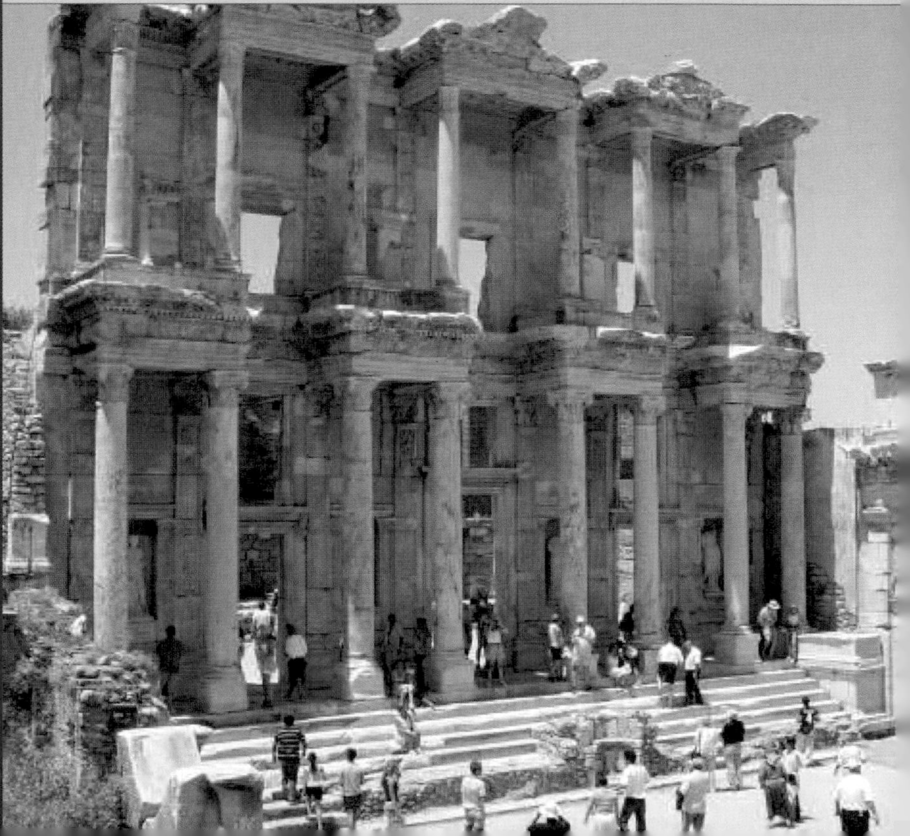

A large theater was carved into the hillside of the acropolis at ancient Pergamum, one of the seven cities of Revelation.

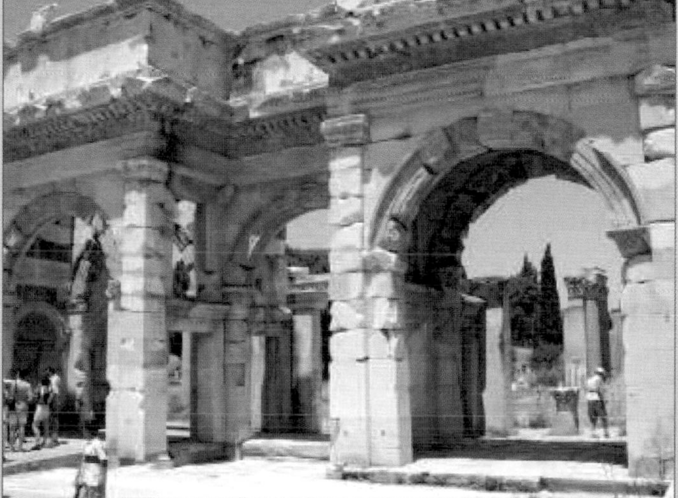

The monumental entrance to the agora (marketplace) at ancient Ephesus.

The Divided Kingdom

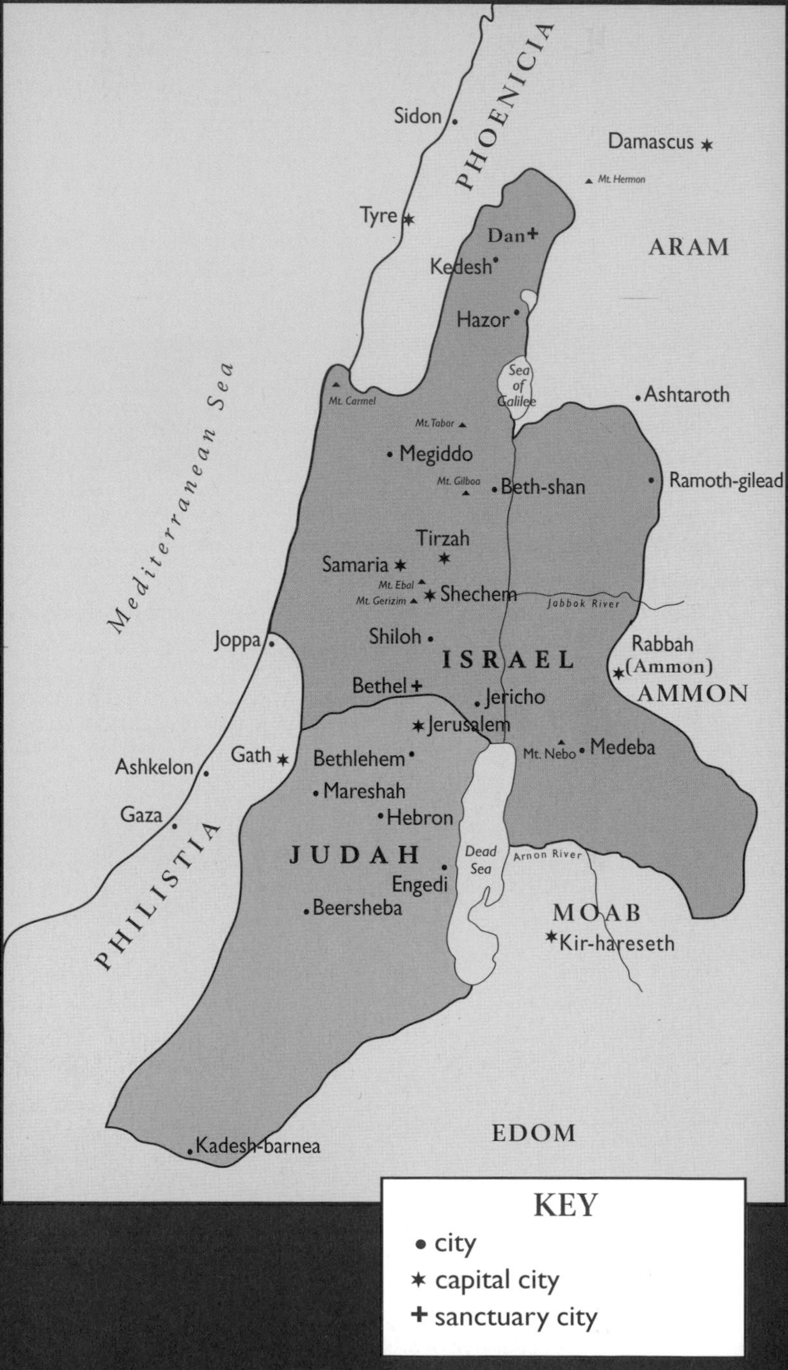

MEGIDDO

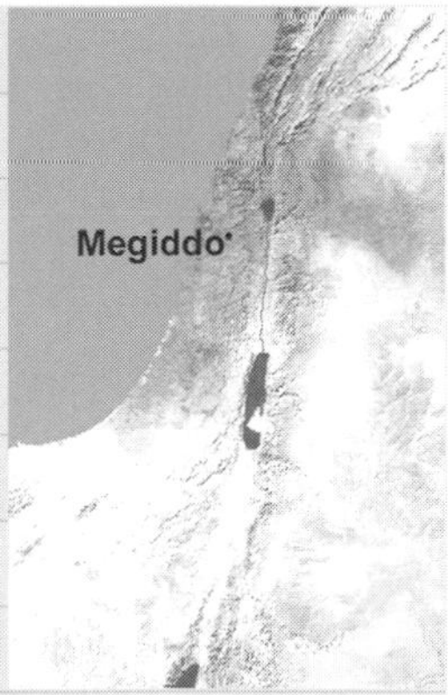

Megiddo lies on the southern end of the Plain of Esdraelon (or the Jezreel Valley), a broad arrowhead-shaped valley. The city of Megiddo was very large, and the site guarded a strategic pass through Mount Carmel. Twenty separate layers of occupation were found at Megiddo, each one built on top of the ruins of the preceding city.

Period of Conquest *Joshua 12:7, 21*—The king of Megiddo was one of thirty-one kings defeated by Joshua during Israel's conquest of Canaan.

Period of the Judges *Judges 1:27*—God allotted the city of Megiddo to the tribe of Manasseh, but they failed to drive the Canaanites out.

Judges 5:19–20—Deborah and Barak defeated Sisera and his armies "by the waters of Megiddo." These waters are the Kishon

Manger and "hitching post" stones at Megiddo, likely from a ninth-century BC stable

River, which flows through the Jezreel Valley (cf. Judg. 5:21). The "river" is normally a small stream. Evidently, part of God's miracle was a sudden thunderstorm that caused the stream to overflow its banks (cf. 5:4).

United Kingdom *1 Kings 4:12*—Solomon placed Beth Shan, Megiddo, and Jezreel under the governorship of Baana, son of Ahilud.

1 Kings 9:15; 10:26—Solomon fortified the city of Megiddo as an important defense post.

Divided Kingdom *2 Kings 9:27*—Jehu attacked King Ahaziah of Judah near Jezreel. Ahaziah managed to flee to Megiddo before he died.

Single Kingdom *2 Kings 23:29–30; 2 Chronicles 35:20–24*—Josiah, the last good king of Judah, unwisely tried to stop Pharaoh Neco and the Egyptian army from marching through the land. Josiah failed and was killed at Megiddo in 609 BC.

Apostolic Age *Revelation 16:13–16*—The last great gathering of armies just before Christ's return to earth will take place at Armageddon. In Hebrew, *Har Megiddo* means the "Hill of Megiddo."

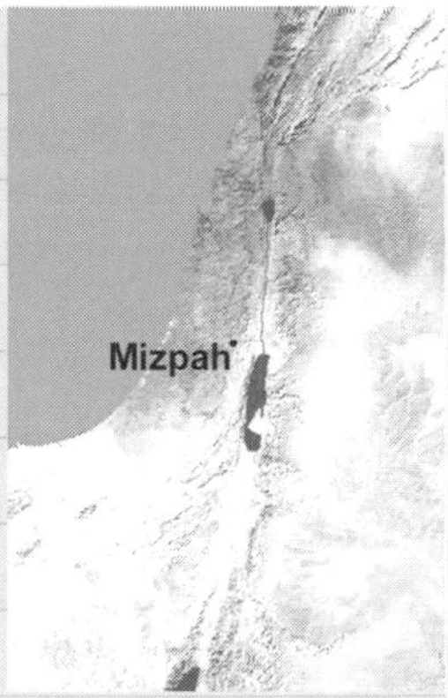

MIZPAH

At least five different cities or towns in the Bible had the name "Mizpah," which means "watchtower." They include (1) Mizpah of Gilead in the Transjordan (present-day northern Jordan) where Jacob and Laban made a covenant (Gen. 31:23–49) and, possibly, where Jephthah the judge later lived (Judg. 11:1, 29, 34); (2) Mizpah in Galilee at the foot of Mount Hermon (Josh. 11:3, 8); (3) Mizpah in Judah in the low foothills near Lachish (Josh. 15:38–39); (4) Mizpah of Moab (present-day central Jordan), where David took his family to protect them from King Saul (1 Sam. 22:3); and (5) Mizpah in Benjamin. This last Mizpah is the one that is most prominent in the Old Testament. The events that occurred there are listed below.

Aerial view of Nebi Samwil, one possible location of Mizpah

Period of Conquest *Joshua 18:26*—God allotted Mizpah to the tribe of Benjamin.

Period of the Judges *Judges 20:1–11*—All Israel gathered at Mizpah to judge the sin of the men of Gibeah. This led to the tragic civil war of Judges 20–21.

1 Samuel 7:5–12—Samuel summoned all Israel to Mizpah for a national convocation to renew their covenant with God. God responded by giving Israel a great victory over the Philistines who mounted an attack against the Israelites.

United Kingdom *1 Samuel 10:17–27*—Samuel summoned Israel to Mizpah a second time to witness the selection of Saul as Israel's first king.

Divided Kingdom *1 Kings 15:16–22; 2 Chronicles 16:1–10*—King Asa of Judah fortified Mizpah to protect against a threatened attack by King Baasha of Israel.

Babylonian Captivity *Jeremiah 40–41*—Mizpah became the seat of government after the destruction of Judah. King Nebuchadnezzar of Babylon appointed Gedaliah governor, and Jeremiah was allowed to live at Mizpah with him. This period ended when Gedaliah was assassinated by a usurper named Ishmael, who took the people of Mizpah captive and forced them to leave.

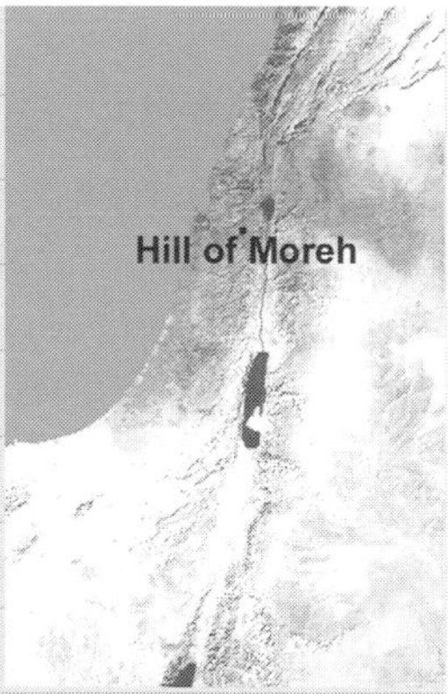

MOREH (HILL OF)

The Hill of Moreh splits the eastern end of the Jezreel Valley. Though less than 1,700 feet high, the hill's strategic location in the valley near the route of the International Highway gave it some prominence. Four villages situated on or near the Hill of Moreh played a significant role in biblical history. These were Ophrah, Shunem, Endor, and Nain.

Period of the Judges *Judges 6:11, 24*—Gideon lived in the town of Ophrah on the southwestern side of the Hill of Moreh in the Jezreel Valley. The modern town of Afula preserves the name of Gideon's hometown.

Judges 7:1—Gideon fought the Midianites, who camped in the Jezreel Valley near the Hill of Moreh.

The Hill of Moreh from Mount Gilboa

United Kingdom *1 Samuel 28:4–8*—The Philistines camped at the village of Shunem on the southern slope of the Hill of Moreh, when they gathered to fight against Saul and the Israelites. Saul secretly visited a medium who lived in Endor, a small village on the northern side of the Hill of Moreh.

1 Kings 1:3–4—Abishag the Shunammite (from the village of Shunem on the southern slope of the Hill of Moreh) was chosen to take care of King David in his old age.

Divided Kingdom *2 Kings 4:8–37*—Elisha often visited the city of Shunem on the Hill of Moreh and stayed with a prominent woman and her husband. He promised the woman she would have a son, and he later raised the woman's young son to life after he had died.

Life of Christ *Luke 7:11–17*—Jesus visited the town of Nain on the northern slope of the Hill of Moreh and raised a woman's young son to life. The people responded by shouting, "A great prophet has appeared among us," possibly remembering the miracle of Elisha that occurred almost nine hundred years earlier in the same general area.

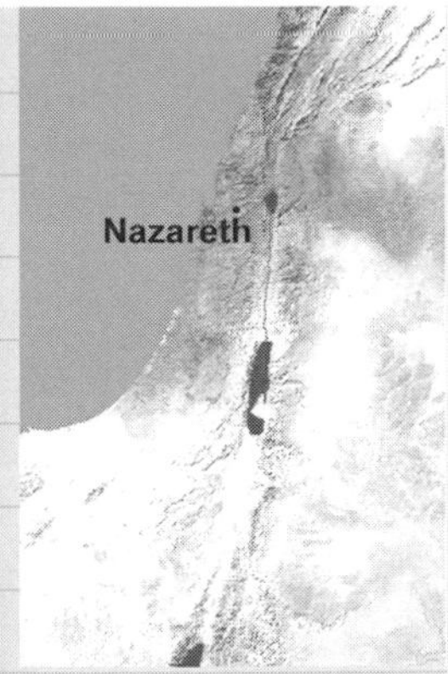

NAZARETH

Nazareth, a small village on a ridge overlooking the Jezreel Valley, is never mentioned in the Old Testament. The name comes from the Hebrew word for branch or shoot (*netzer*). Nazareth became important historically because it was the "hometown" of Jesus.

Life of Christ *Luke 1:26–33*—The angel Gabriel appeared to Mary in Nazareth and announced that she would be the mother of Jesus.

Luke 2:1–7—Joseph and Mary left Nazareth and went to Bethlehem, where Jesus was born.

Matthew 2:21–23—After fleeing to Egypt to escape Herod's decree to murder the children of Bethlehem, Joseph, Mary, and Jesus returned to the land and settled in Nazareth.

Luke 2:41–52—Jesus' boyhood and young manhood were spent in Nazareth, though every year "his parents went to Jerusalem for the Feast of the Passover."

Luke 4:16–30—After Jesus' baptism in the Jordan River and temptation in the wilderness, He preached His first recorded sermon at Nazareth. The people of Nazareth responded angrily to Jesus' message and tried to kill Him by throwing Him from the "Mount of Precipice."

Mark 6:1–6—On a later visit to Nazareth, Jesus could perform few miracles because of the persistent unbelief of the people.

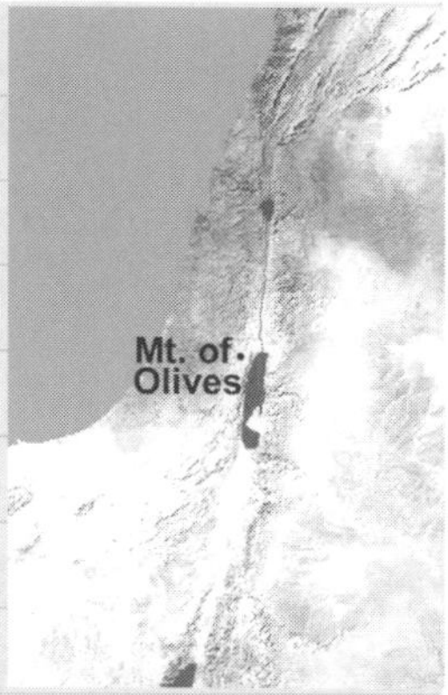

OLIVES (MOUNT OF)

The Mount of Olives rises to the east of Jerusalem and reaches a height of almost 2,500 feet. Although never part of Jerusalem proper, the Mount of Olives is inseparably linked to Jerusalem geographically and historically. The hill received its name because it was covered with olive groves. Though some olive trees still remain, today the hill is largely covered with Jewish graves and Christian shrines.

The western slopes of the Mount of Olives on which Jesus gave His Olivet Disc

United Kingdom *2 Samuel 15:30–37*—King David walked up the Mount of Olives as he fled Jerusalem to escape from his son Absalom. He was "weeping as he went; his head was covered and he was barefoot."

1 Kings 11:7–8—Solomon built pagan shrines for his many wives on the southern portion of the Mount of Olives.

Single Kingdom *Ezekiel 11:22–23*—Ezekiel witnessed the glory of the Lord leave Solomon's temple and Jerusalem by way of the Mount of Olives.

Babylonian Captivity *Ezekiel 43:1–5*—Ezekiel described the glory of the Lord returning from the east (over the Mount of Olives) to enter a new temple.

Restoration *Zechariah 14:3–5*—Zechariah described a day when the Lord's feet would stand on the Mount of Olives and the mountain would be split in two.

Life of Christ *Matthew 21:1–11; Mark 11:1–10; Luke 19:28–40; John 12:12–16*—Jesus rode down the Mount of Olives into Jerusalem on a donkey for His "triumphal entry."

Luke 19:41–44—Jesus wept over Jerusalem from the Mount of Olives.

Matthew 24–25; Mark 13:1–37; Luke 21:5–36—Jesus described the prophetic future of Jerusalem to His disciples while they were seated on the Mount of Olives.

Matthew 26:36–56; Mark 14:32–52; Luke 22:39–53; John 18:1–11—Jesus and His disciples left the upper room and went to the garden of Gethsemane on the Mount of Olives. Here Jesus was arrested.

Luke 24:50–53; Acts 1:9–12—Jesus, after His resurrection, ascended to heaven from the Mount of Olives.

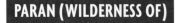

PARAN (WILDERNESS OF)

The Wilderness of Paran straddles the central part of the Sinai peninsula, south of the Wilderness of Zin. While the boundaries are not well defined, it is generally located between the Arabah on the east and the Wilderness of Shur on the west. The desert oasis of Kadesh Barnea bordered both the Wilderness of Paran and the Wilderness of Zin.

Patriarchal Period *Genesis 14:6*—Kedorlaomer, one of the four kings who attacked Sodom and Gomorrah, conquered as far as El Paran near the desert.

Genesis 21:21—When Hagar was driven out of the household of Abraham, she and Ishmael fled to the Wilderness of Paran.

Period of the Exodus *Numbers 10:12; 12:16; 13:3, 26*—The children of Israel wandered through the Wilderness of Paran from Mount Sinai. Moses sent out the twelve spies to explore the land from Kadesh-barnea in the Wilderness of Paran.

The nation of Israel spent part of its wilderness wanderings in the Wilderness of Paran.

QUMRAN

Qumran is located near the northwestern shore of the Dead Sea and was the site of a small settlement that existed during the time of Christ. The Dead Sea Scrolls were discovered near Qumran in 1947, and it was the discovery of these scrolls that gave the site its importance. Many (though not all) scholars believe Qumran was inhabited by a Jewish sect called the Essenes. Most likely the Essenes, hearing of the approach of the Roman armies in AD 68, placed their scrolls in pottery jars and hid them in the nearby caves, intending to return for them later. The Essenes then joined the rebels who captured Masada. They remained at Masada, where they were killed by the Romans in AD 73.

A cave at Qumran where some of the Dead Sea Scrolls were discovered

RAMAH

Ramah, a strategic village about six miles north of Jerusalem, guarded an important crossroads in the territory of Benjamin. The city sat on the "Way of the Patriarchs," the internal road running through the hill country of Israel, where it intersected the main east–west road that ran from the Mediterranean coast through the hill country to Jericho.

Period of Conquest *Joshua 18:25*—God allotted Ramah to the tribe of Benjamin.

Period of the Judges *Judges 4:5*—The prophetess Deborah sat under a palm tree between Ramah and Bethel to judge Israel.

1 Samuel 1:1–20; 7:15–17—Elkanah and Hannah resided in Ramah (also called Ramathaim). The prophet Samuel was born in Ramah and lived in Ramah as an adult.

1 Samuel 8:4; 9:6, 27; 10:1—The people came to Samuel at Ramah to ask for a king. Later, Samuel privately anointed Saul as king in Ramah.

United Kingdom *1 Samuel 19:18–20:1*—David fled from Saul and visited Samuel at Ramah. Saul pursued David but God intervened to spare him.

1 Samuel 25:1; 28:3—After his death, Samuel was buried in Ramah.

Divided Kingdom *1 Kings 15:16–22; 2 Chronicles 16:1–6*—King Baasha of Israel captured and fortified Ramah to block access to Jerusalem. The blockade was lifted and the building materials were removed by King Asa of Judah.

Single Kingdom *Isaiah 10:29; Hosea 5:8*—The inhabitants of Ramah fled in terror when the Assyrian army marched on Jerusalem in 701 BC. Ramah fell to Sennacherib and the Assyrians.

Babylonian Captivity *Jeremiah 31:15; 40:1*—The Babylonians used Ramah as their "staging area" after the fall of Jerusalem. Captives were taken there for processing before being deported to Babylon. Jeremiah described the women who watched their children being taken into captivity from Ramah as "Rachel weeping for her children."

Restoration *Ezra 2:26; Nehemiah 7:30*—Some of the remnant who returned from the Babylonian captivity reinhabited Ramah.

SAMARIA/SEBASTE

The city of Samaria was the final capital of the northern kingdom of Israel. Its strategic location allowed the kings of Israel to exert control out to the Mediterranean coast and the International Highway while protecting key routes into Israel. The city of Samaria was destroyed by the Assyrians in 721 BC.

Divided Kingdom *1 Kings 16:23–24*—King Omri of Israel moved his capital to the city of Samaria.

1 Kings 16:32—King Ahab built a temple for Baal in Samaria and erected an altar for Baal in the temple.

1 Kings 20:1–21—God delivered Samaria from attack by Ben-Hadad, king of Aram.

1 Kings 22:1–40—Ahab and Jehoshaphat met in Samaria to plan an attack against Ramoth Gilead. Micaiah the prophet predicted failure. Ahab was killed in battle and carried back to Samaria for burial. His chariot was washed out by the Pool of Samaria. Dogs licked up his blood, fulfilling Micaiah's prophecy.

2 Kings 1:2–17—King Ahaziah of Israel fell through the lattice in the upper chamber of his palace in Samaria and died.

2 Kings 6:8–23—The Arameans came to Dothan to capture Elisha, but God blinded them. Elisha led the army to Samaria, where their sight was restored.

2 Kings 6:24–7:20—The Arameans besieged Samaria and a great famine ensued. God delivered the city from the army and provided food for the inhabitants.

2 Kings 10:1–7—Ahab's seventy sons were slaughtered in Samaria, and their heads were sent to King Jehu in Jezreel.

2 Kings 17:3–16—The Assyrians besieged, captured, and destroyed the city of Samaria.

Hosea 7:1; 8:5–6; 10:5–7—The prophet Hosea predicted God's judgment against Samaria for the people's idolatry.

Amos 3:12; 4:1; 6:1—The prophet Amos predicted God's judgment against Samaria for the people's social inequities.

Micah 1:1, 5–7—The prophet Micah predicted God's destruction of the city of Samaria, promising God would "pour her stones into the valley."

Babylonian Captivity *Jeremiah 41:5*—Gedaliah, the governor placed over Judah by the Babylonians after Jerusalem's fall, was murdered by Ishmael. The next day Ishmael also murdered seventy pilgrims from Shechem, Shiloh, and Samaria who were coming to Jerusalem to mourn the destruction of the temple.

Intertestamental Era Alexander the Great conquered Samaria in 332 BC. The city was completely destroyed in 108 BC by John Hyrcanus, who forced the inhabitants to convert to Judaism. Herod the Great later rebuilt the city and renamed it Sebaste in honor of the Roman emperor, Augustus Caesar. (Sebaste is the Greek translation of the Latin word *Augustus*.)

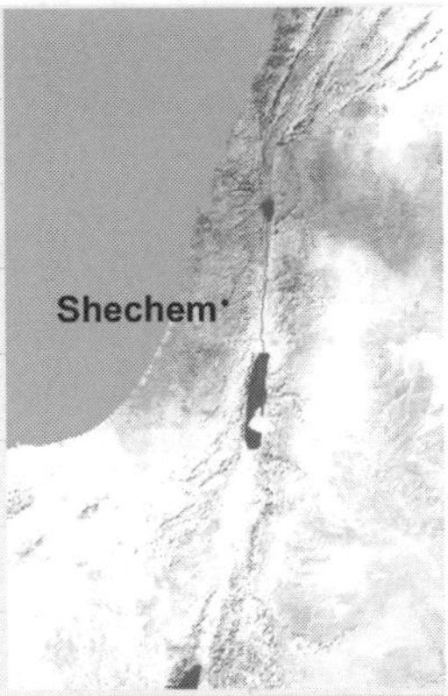

SHECHEM

Shechem, a key city in the hill country of Ephraim, played a central role in Israel's religious and civil history. Nestled between Mount Ebal and Mount Gerizim, the city watched a parade of historical giants, from Abraham to Jacob to Joshua to Jesus, pass through. After the destruction of Jerusalem in AD 70, a new city was established here for veterans of the Roman army. The city, named Neapolis ("new city"), gave its name to the present-day city of Nablus. For more information see Ebal (Mount) and Gerizim (Mount).

Patriarchal Period *Genesis 12:6*—Abram's first stop in the Promised Land was Shechem.

Genesis 33:18–19—Jacob's first stop when he returned to the Promised Land was Shechem.

Genesis 34:1–31—Jacob's daughter, Dinah, was raped in Shechem. Her brothers avenged her by killing the men of the city.

Period of the Exodus *Deuteronomy 27:4–13*—Moses commanded the Israelites to gather on Mount Ebal and Mount Gerizim to recite the blessings and cursings of the covenant. (Shechem is between Ebal and Gerizim.)

Period of Conquest *Joshua 8:30–35*—Joshua gathered Israel on Mount Ebal and Mount Gerizim to recite the blessings and cursings of the covenant.

Joshua 17:7; 1 Chronicles 7:28—Shechem, while near the border with Manasseh, was allotted to the tribe of Ephraim.

Joshua 20:1–9; 1 Chronicles 6:67—Shechem was designated as one of the six cities of refuge in the land of Israel.

Joshua 24:1–28—Joshua gathered all Israel to Shechem to renew their covenant with the Lord.

Joshua 24:32—Israel buried the bones of Joseph in Shechem at the plot of ground purchased by Jacob.

Period of the Judges *Judges 9:1–57*—Abimelech, Gideon's son from a concubine who lived in Shechem (8:31), became Israel's first "king," although his rule was not sanctioned by the Lord. He ruled from Shechem, and he died in Shechem fighting his own people.

United Kingdom *Psalms 60:6; 108:7*—King David affirmed God's ownership and control over portions of Israel, including Shechem.

Divided Kingdom *1 Kings 12:1–24; 2 Chronicles 10:1–19*—Rehoboam went to Shechem to be crowned king of all Israel. His harsh response to the northern tribes caused them to rebel against his authority.

1 Kings 12:25—The first capital of the northern kingdom of Israel was established at Shechem.

Babylonian Captivity *Jeremiah 41:1–8*—Gedaliah, the governor placed over Judah by the Babylonians after Jerusalem's fall, was murdered by Ishmael. The next day Ishmael also murdered seventy pilgrims from Shechem, Shiloh, and Samaria who were coming to Jerusalem to mourn the destruction of the temple.

Life of Christ *John 4:1–42*—Jesus met the Samaritan woman at Jacob's well, near the ancient site of Shechem.

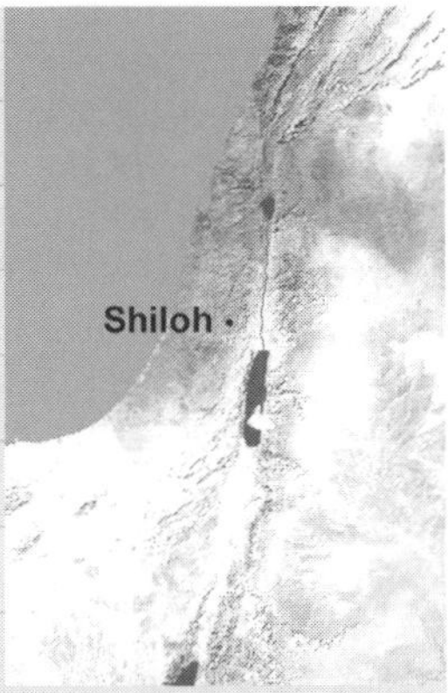

SHILOH

Shiloh became the first religious center for the tribes of Israel after they entered the land of Israel. The site's isolated, remote location gave it security, and its location in the central hills gave it accessibility to the entire nation.

Period of Conquest *Joshua 18:1, 8–10*—Joshua gathered the Israelites to the Tent of Meeting at Shiloh. The remaining land allotments for the tribes were made at Shiloh.

Joshua 22:10–12—All Israel gathered at Shiloh to go to war against the tribes east of the Jordan River for setting up an altar. War was averted when the tribes explained the meaning of the altar.

Period of the Judges *Judges 21:15–22*—The men from the tribe of Benjamin went to Shiloh to "capture" brides after their tribe was nearly destroyed in war. In describing the event, the writer gives an exact description of Shiloh's location "to the north of Bethel, and east of the road that goes from Bethel to Shechem, and to the south of Lebonah."

1 Samuel 1:3–20—At Shiloh, Hannah prayed for a son and gave birth to Samuel.

After entering Promised Lan Israel erected God's taberna at Shiloh.

1 Samuel 2:11–26—Samuel was dedicated to the Lord at Shiloh and remained at Shiloh to minister before the Lord with Eli the priest. Eli's wicked sons displeased God at Shiloh.

1 Samuel 3:1–21—God appeared to Samuel at Shiloh and announced the destruction of Eli's family because of sin.

1 Samuel 4:1–22—Eli's sons took the ark from Shiloh, and it was captured by the Philistines. On hearing the news, Eli died in Shiloh. Although not mentioned directly in the Bible, it is likely that the various elements of the tabernacle were scattered throughout Israel at this time. Shiloh was abandoned by Israel or destroyed by the Philistines.

Divided Kingdom *1 Kings 14:1–13*—When King Jeroboam's son became ill, Jeroboam disguised his wife and sent her to Shiloh to visit the prophet Ahijah. Ahijah announced the child would die because of Jeroboam's sin.

Psalm 78:60—The psalmist described how God "abandoned the tabernacle of Shiloh" because of Israel's idolatry.

Single Kingdom *Jeremiah 7:12–14; 26:4–9*—The prophet Jeremiah used God's destruction of the tabernacle at Shiloh as an object lesson to judge the people of Jerusalem for idolatry.

Babylonian Captivity *Jeremiah 41:1–8*—Gedaliah, the governor placed over Judah by the Babylonians after Jerusalem's fall, was murdered by Ishmael. The next day Ishmael also murdered seventy pilgrims from Shechem, Shiloh, and Samaria who were coming to Jerusalem to mourn the destruction of the temple.

TABGHA

Tabgha is the site of several springs on the northwestern shore of the Sea of Galilee. The Arabic name comes from the Greek word *heptapegon*, which means "seven springs." These springs flow into the Sea of Galilee and provide a warm-water environment, especially in the winter, making the area one of the major fishing sites on the sea. This location has traditionally been identified as the site where Jesus performed the feeding of the five thousand (Mark 6:30–44). However, Luke 9:10 and John 6:1 seem to indicate that Jesus performed this miracle on the eastern side of the Sea of Galilee beyond the city of Bethsaida. While Tabgha is not the site where the feeding of the five thousand occurred, it is the likely spot where Jesus met with His disciples when they were fishing.

Life of Christ *Matthew 4:18–24; Mark 1:16–20; Luke 5:1–11*—Jesus called His disciples from their fishing boats to follow Him. They were now to become "fishers of men."

John 21:1–24—Following His resurrection, Jesus appeared to Peter and the other disciples along the shore of Galilee after they had experienced a long night of unproductive fishing. He instructed them to cast their nets on the right side of the boat, resulting in a large catch of fish. Jesus restored Peter from the shame of his prior denials and tested the depth of his love by asking three times, "Do you love me?" Here Jesus also commissioned Peter to "feed my sheep."

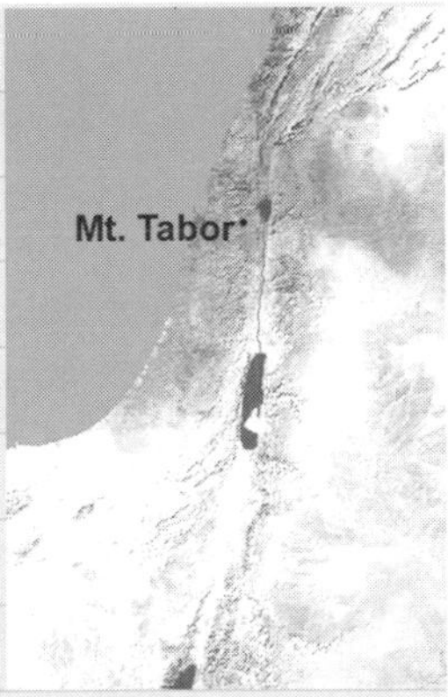

TABOR (MOUNT)

Mount Tabor rises in majestic isolation from the floor of the Jezreel Valley. This single peak soars to a height of 1,850 feet and towers over the International Highway at the point where the highway leaves the Jezreel Valley on its journey north toward the Sea of Galilee. Mount Tabor is the traditional site of the transfiguration, although Mount Hermon may be a better candidate.

Period of Conquest *Joshua 19:12, 22, 34*—Mount Tabor served as a boundary point between the tribes of Zebulun, Issachar, and Naphtali.

Mount Tabor, located a few miles southeast of Nazareth

1 Chronicles 6:77—God allotted Mount Tabor as a special city for the Levites.

Period of the Judges *Judges 4:6, 12–16*—Deborah and Barak gathered the army of Israel to Mount Tabor to fight against the army of Jabin, king of Hazor. Jabin's army was led by his general, Sisera.

Judges 8:18–21—Gideon killed the leaders of the Midianites because they had earlier slaughtered Gideon's brothers on Mount Tabor.

Single Kingdom *Psalm 89:12*—The psalmist used the heights of Mount Tabor and Mount Hermon to describe God's exalted creation.

Jeremiah 46:18—The prophet Jeremiah compared the grandeur of Nebuchadnezzar to the exalted height of Mount Tabor or Mount Carmel.

Life of Christ *Matthew 17:1–9; Mark 9:2–9; Luke 9:28–37*—Mount Tabor is the traditional site of the "Mount of Transfiguration," although Mount Hermon is more likely the actual location.

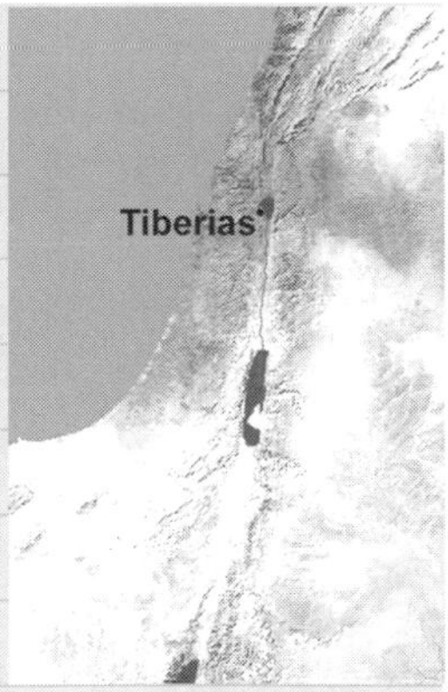

TIBERIAS

The city of Tiberias was founded by Herod Antipas in AD 17–20 and was named after Tiberias Caesar, the emperor of Rome (AD 14–37). Tiberias was the emperor when Jesus began His public ministry (Luke 3:1). This city also gave its name to the Sea of Tiberias (i.e., the Sea of Galilee). There is no record that Jesus visited Tiberias. The area was known for its therapeutic hot springs, and this may explain in part why large numbers of sick people came to Jesus for healing when He was in the area.

Life of Christ *Matthew 11:20–24*—Jesus predicted judgment for several towns around the Sea of Galilee—Korazin, Bethsaida, and Capernaum—and they are gone. He did not pronounce judgment on Tiberias, and it remains.

John 6:1; 21:1—Jesus ministered on the Sea of Tiberias, and curious residents sailed their boats from Tiberias to witness His miracles.

Modern hotels crowd the shoreline of Tiberias.

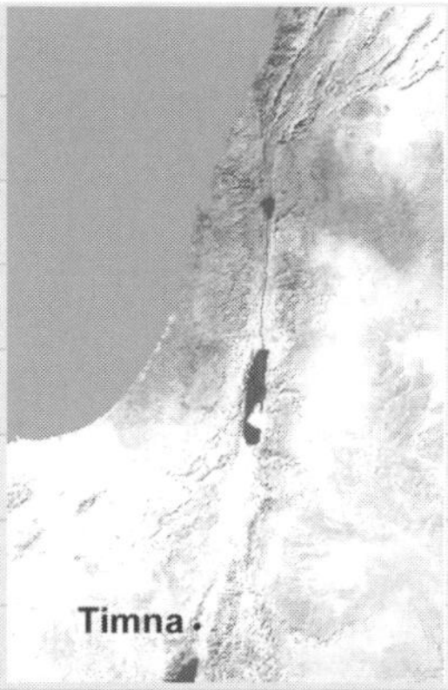

TIMNA

Timna is a fascinating geological area about twenty miles north of modern Eilat. The copper mines of Timna date back to the time of the ancient Egyptians. The site also contains an amazing natural sandstone formation named "Solomon's pillars"—although it has no historical connection to King Solomon. In recent years a full-scale model of Israel's original tabernacle has been on display in Timna.

Model of Israel's tabernacle on display at Tir

ZIN (WILDERNESS OF)

The Wilderness of Zin was located on the southern boundary of the Promised Land, on the northeast side of the Wilderness of Paran. The desert oasis of Kadesh-barnea bordered both the Wilderness of Zin and the Wilderness of Paran.

Period of the Exodus *Numbers 13:21*—The twelve spies were sent to explore the Promised Land from the Wilderness of Zin.

Numbers 20:1–13; 27:14; 33:36; Deuteronomy 32:51—The children of Israel wandered through the Wilderness of Zin during their forty years in the desert. It was at Kadesh in the Wilderness of Zin where Moses disobeyed God and was not allowed to enter the Promised Land.

Numbers 34:3–4—God established the Wilderness of Zin as part of Israel's southern border.

One of the many deep canyons in the Wadi Zin

PART THREE

The Land of Egypt

- The Gods of Egypt
- Hieroglyphics
- I Want My Mummy
- A Brief History of Egypt Through the Time of David and Solomon

THE GODS OF EGYPT

At the time of the Exodus, God vowed that He would "go through the land of Egypt" to "strike down all the firstborn in the land" (Ex. 12:12 NASB). One reason for this climactic judgment was to bring about God's judgment "against all the gods of Egypt" so that all would know He alone was God. (See also Numbers 33:4.)

The Egyptians worshiped a pantheon of gods and goddesses. Some of the major ones included the following:

- Amun/Amun Re, the chief god of the New Kingdom
- Anubis, god of the netherworld with the head of a jackal
- Apis, ancient bull god associated with the city of Memphis
- Aten, the sun disk as the sole deity, adopted by Akhenaton in 1372–1353 BC
- Heqet, goddess of childbirth, pictured as a woman with a frog's head or as a frog
- Horakhte/Harakhty, "Horus of the horizon" or "Horus the Younger," an early national god associated with both Horus and Re and represented with a falcon's head on which is a sun disk
- Horus, the earliest national god of Egypt. The pharaoh was believed to be the incarnation of Horus, which was represented as a falcon.
- Isis, wife of Osiris and mother of Horus who represented motherhood, children, medicine, and love
- Maat, the daughter of Re who was the goddess of truth, justice, and cosmic order
- Nut, the sky goddess
- Osiris, god of the underworld

- Re, early Egyptian sun god, pictured as a falcon-headed man with the sun disk

- Thoth, the god of wisdom, learning, time, and measurement. He is pictured as an ibis or a baboon and holding writing materials.

HIEROGLYPHICS

Egyptian tomb painting showing a herdsman

The term "hieroglyphics" comes from two Greek words meaning "sacred writings." Hieroglyphics is the ancient Egyptian system of writing that used pictures to represent sounds. In 1799 the French discovered a monumental inscription written in three languages—Hieroglyphics, Demotic, and Greek. This inscription, called the Rosetta stone because of its discovery in the Egyptian port city of Rosetta, provided initial clues to help begin the process of translating hieroglyphics. But it was Jean-François Champollion of France who finally discovered the proper way to translate the hieroglyphic text in 1822.

The Rosetta stone is currently on display in the British Museum.

I WANT MY MUMMY

Many people are fascinated by the mummification process practiced in ancient Egypt. At the time of death, the person to be mummified was taken to the place of purification where the body was first washed in a solution of natron (a naturally occurring compound of sodium carbonate and sodium bicarbonate). After this initial cleansing, the body was then taken to the house of beauty for the actual mummification process.

The liver, lungs, stomach, and intestines were removed and placed in canopic jars. The lids of these jars were often decorated with images representing the four sons of Horus. Once the internal organs were removed, the corpse was packed with natron to dehydrate it. After forty days the embalmers repacked the body with clean natron and wrapped it in linen wrappings soaked in resin and aromatic oils.

The entire process from death to burial took seventy days. The mummification portion took forty days, and it took an additional fifteen days to wrap the body. During that time the tomb was prepared with everything the deceased would need in the afterlife.

The burials of Israel's patriarchs, Jacob and Joseph, followed Egypt's mummification procedures.

- "When Jacob had finished giving instructions to his sons, he drew his feet up into the bed, breathed his last and was gathered to his people. Joseph threw himself upon his father and wept over him and kissed him. Then Joseph directed the physicians in his service to embalm his father Israel. So the physicians embalmed him, taking a full forty days, for that was the time required for embalming. And the Egyptians mourned for him seventy days" (Gen. 49:33–50:3).

- "So Joseph died at the age of a hundred and ten. And after they embalmed him, he was placed in a coffin in Egypt" (Gen. 50:26).

A BRIEF HISTORY OF EGYPT THROUGH THE TIME OF DAVID AND SOLOMON

Egypt has a long and glorious history. Unfortunately, that history confuses many visitors who struggle to match up pharaohs and their monuments with specific events in the Bible. These pages will present a broad sweep of Egypt's history, from the beginning of Egypt through the time of Kings David and Solomon of Israel, and King Rehoboam of Judah. The biblical connections are identified using the symbol .

Protodynastic Period (Dynasties I–II, 3100–2700 BC) *Egypt United*

- Menes (also called Narmer) united Upper and Lower Egypt

and became Egypt's first pharaoh.

- His capital was Memphis, at the meeting point of the two kingdoms.

Old Kingdom Period (Dynasties III–VI, 2700–2200 BC)
The Pyramid Age

- Djoser, the first king of the Third Dynasty, built the Step Pyramid at Saqqara.
- Khufu, the second king of the Fourth Dynasty, built the Great Pyramid at Giza.
- Kafre, Khufu's successor, built the Second Pyramid and the Sphinx at Giza.
- Menkure, Khafre's successor, built the Third Pyramid at Giza.

First Intermediate Period (Dynasties VII–XI, 2200–1991 BC) *Period of Feudalism*

- Abraham traveled to Egypt during this period (Gen. 12:10–20).

Middle Kingdom Period (Dynasty XII, 1991–1786 BC)
Era of Expansion

- In 1898 BC Joseph was sold into slavery.
- In 1885 BC Joseph stood before Pharaoh.
- In 1876 BC Israel moved to Egypt.
- In 1805 BC Joseph died.

Second Intermediate Period (Dynasties XIII–XVII, 1786–1570 BC)
Hyksos Invasion

- The Israelites likely fared well under Hyksos rule since they were fellow Semites.

New Kingdom Period (Dynasties XVIII–XX, 1570–1090 BC) *Egypt's Golden Age*

Eighteenth Dynasty (Dynasty XVIII, 1570–1304 BC)

- **Amosis** (1570–1546 BC) drove out the Hyksos and united Egypt. Amosis is likely the pharaoh of Exodus 1:8. ("Then a new king, who did not know about Joseph, came to power in Egypt.")

- **Amenhotep I** (1546–1526 BC) consolidated the land. Amenhotep I or his father instituted the repressive policies against the Israelites (Ex. 1:11–14).

- **Thutmose I** (1526–1512 BC) conquered Nubia as far as the fourth cataract and led an expedition to Canaan and Syria. His burial was the first in the Valley of the Kings.

  Thutmose I is the pharaoh who ordered the midwives to kill the male Israelite children (Ex. 1:15–22). Moses was born about 1526 BC, at the beginning of the reign of Thutmose I. The "daughter of Pharaoh" who discovered Moses in the ark would have been Hatshepsut (see Hatshepsut below).

- **Thutmose II** (1512–1504 BC) was the son of Thutmose I through a concubine. He married Hatshepsut, who was his half sister and the daughter of Thutmose I by his official wife. After a short reign he died, leaving only a girl by Hatshepsut.

- **Hatshepsut** (1504–1482 BC) was the daughter of Thutmose I and was married to both Thutmose II and Thutmose III. Thutmose III was very young when his father died. Hatshepsut ruled as coregent with him, but she maintained so much control that he was not able to reign as king until after her death. She even pictured herself as a man with a ceremonial beard.

  Moses would have become forty in 1486. Thutmose III, by now trying to regain the throne from his mother/wife Hatshepsut, would have used the opportunity of Moses' murder of an Egyptian to try to kill off a potential rival to the throne and get back at Hatshepsut. ("When Pharaoh heard of this, he tried to kill Moses" [Ex. 2:15].)

▪ **Thutmose III** (1504–1450 BC) was the son of Thutmose II through a secondary wife. Thutmose III also married Hatshepsut to legitimize his title to the throne. He only ruled as supreme king following her death in 1482 BC. Her attempt to usurp him so enraged him that, following her death, he effaced all of her monuments and tried to erase any memory of her existence. He conducted numerous military campaigns and established Egypt as the supreme power throughout all Canaan.

The death of Thutmose III prompted God's calling of Moses at the burning bush. ("During that long period, the king of Egypt died. The Israelites groaned in their slavery and cried out, and their cry for help because of their slavery went up to God" [Ex. 2:23].)

▪ **Amenhotep II** (1450–1425 BC) was the son of Thutmose III and was known for his physical prowess. If the Exodus took place in 1446 BC, then Amenhotep II was the pharaoh of the Exodus.

▪ **Thutmose IV** (1425–1408 BC) followed his father to the throne. A stela found between the legs of the Sphinx recorded that he dug the Sphinx out of the sand while a youth and was rewarded with a promise that he would someday be king. The "Dream Stela" could be indirect confirmation of the death of Pharaoh's firstborn son (Ex. 12:29–30) since Thutmose IV would not have needed such a promise had he been the first-born.

▪ **Amenhotep III** (1408–1372 BC) was the ruler when the Eighteenth Dynasty reached its greatest splendor territorially and artistically. The "Colossi of Memnon," each standing sixty-five feet high, were statues of Amenhotep III. His was a reign of relative peace and prosperity. However, there were signs of trouble. The Amarna tablets begin during this period. Israel would have entered the Promised Land during the reign of Amenhotep III.

▪ **Amenhotep IV** (Akhenaton) (1372–1353 BC) brought a major change in Egypt. He abandoned the gods of his fathers and tried to promote the worship of Aten, the solar disk that he perceived as the source of all blessing. He also moved the capital of Egypt from Luxor to Amarna, and he involved himself more in religious contemplation than in international affairs.

The Amarna tablets mention the invasion of Canaan by the Habiru/Hapiru. Though the word cannot be directly equated with "Hebrew" because it was used earlier than the formation of the Hebrew nation, it referred to nomadic tribesmen that could include the people of Israel.

- **Smenkhkare** (1355–1352 BC) was a minor pharaoh. He had a brief coregency with his father-in-law, and he died shortly after Akhenaton.

- **Tutankhatin/Tutankhamen** (1352–1344 BC) was another son-in-law of Akhenaton. Although he was a minor pharaoh, two major events are associated with him. First, there was a religious revolt during his reign when the forces loyal to the old god Amun overthrew those trying to continue the religious reforms of Akhenaton. The change in Tut's name (from "atin" to "amen") reflects his bowing to the pressures of the religious majority. Second, he is the only pharaoh whose completely unopened tomb has been discovered. The objects found in the tomb are priceless and provide an excellent glimpse into the splendor that must have been part of the royal court.

- **Ay/Eye** (1344–1340 BC) After Tutankhamen's death, his wife sent to the king of the Hittites and asked that one of his sons marry her. The king sent a son, but he was murdered shortly after arriving in Egypt. It is possible that Ay, a high official in Tutankhamen's court, heard of the queen's plans and arranged for the murder. He became pharaoh but had only a short reign before he died.

- **Haremhab** (1340–1304 BC) was a general who assumed control after the death of Ay. He prepared the way for the advances of the Nineteenth Dynasty.

Nineteenth Dynasty (Dynasty XIX, 1304–1200 BC)

- **Rameses I** (1304–1303 BC) was an army officer under Haremhab. He was older when he assumed the throne, and he only reigned for a short time.

- **Seti I** (1303–1290 BC) was Rameses' son. Seti began reestablishing Egypt's empire in Syria and Canaan.

- **Rameses II** (1290–1224 BC) succeeded Seti to the throne and fought a number of battles in Canaan. He confronted the Hittites in the famous battle at Kadesh on the Orontes River. Some believe that Rameses II was the pharaoh of the Exodus.

- **Merneptah** (1224–1214 BC) was the son of Rameses II. He fought in Canaan to preserve the empire of his father, and he recorded his campaign on a stela called the "Hymn of Victory of Merneptah."

  The Merneptah stela is significant because it names Israel as one of the nations he has subdued. ("Israel is laid waste, his seed is not.") It is dated to the fifth year of Merneptah's reign (ca. 1220 BC), indicating that the people of Israel were in the land and recognized as a legitimate entity by this time. This poses problems for those who would date the Exodus to the time of Rameses II.

- **Seti II** (1214–1208 BC)

- **Siptah** (1208–1202 BC)

- **Twosre** (1202–1200 BC)

Twentieth Dynasty (Dynasty XX, 1200–1085 BC)

- **Sethnakht** (1200–1197 BC) deposed the last king of the Nineteenth Dynasty and began a new dynasty.

- **Rameses III** (1197–1165 BC) was the last great king of the New Kingdom. He stopped the threatened invasion of Egypt by the Sea-peoples.

  Some of these invaders were called the Peleste. They later settled on the coast of Canaan and became the Philistines of the later period of Judges and 1 Samuel.

- **Rameses IV–Rameses XI** (1165–1085 BC). The New Kingdom underwent a rapid decline during this period.

Period of Decline (Dynasties XXI–XXIV, 1085–715 BC)

Twenty-first Dynasty (Dynasty XXI, 1085–950 BC)

- Egypt suffered through a period of weakness with double rulerships at Tanis and Thebes. This rivalry sapped Egypt's strength and made her a minor player in the international scene.

  During this period David and Solomon ruled a united Israel. Neither king was threatened by attack from Egypt, though Solomon did make an alliance with Egypt by marrying Pharaoh's daughter (1 Kings 3:1).

Twenty-second Dynasty (Dynasty XXII, 950–730 BC)

- Egypt was again united under Libyan military officers who established their capital in Herakleopolis. This dynasty is called the Libyan dynasty. It had several contacts with Israel and Judah.

- Sheshonk/Shishak ascended to the throne in 950 BC. In 927 BC Shishak invaded Judah and Israel during the reigns of King Rehoboam of Judah and King Jeroboam of Israel (1 Kings 14:25–28).

ASWAN

Aswan, called Swenet by the ancient Egyptians, marked the southern end of Egypt at the first cataract (set of rapids) of the Nile River. From this region the Egyptians quarried the granite used in many of their temples. Aswan was also the gateway to the caravan routes that led south to Sudan and Nubia. In the time of the Ptolemies, the town became known as Syene, and the granite quarried here was known as syenite.

South of the city of Aswan is the Aswan High Dam, built between 1960 and 1971 by Egypt and the Soviet Union. The damming of the Nile by the High Dam formed Lake Nasser, an immense lake named for former Egyptian President Gamal Abdel Nasser.

The Isis temple that originally stood on the island of Philae was dismantled and moved to higher ground to save it from the lake formed by the Aswan Dam.

GIZA

The Giza plateau, rising on the western bank of the Nile River across from Cairo, was part of the necropolis of ancient Memphis. Here the pharaohs of the Fourth Dynasty built the imposing pyramids, one of the seven wonders of the ancient world, and the Sphinx.

The largest of the pyramids is the Pyramid of Cheops, or Khufu. According to Herodotus (*History* 2.124–25), it took a hundred thousand men, working in shifts of three months per year, twenty years to build this pyramid. It stands 450 feet high.

The Sphinx with the pyramid of Khafre in the di

The second pyramid is that of Khafre, or Chephren, standing 448 feet high. This is also the pharaoh who is thought to have built the Sphinx. The Sphinx has a lion's body with a human face, possibly that of the pharaoh himself. Carved from the natural rock outcropping, the Sphinx is 241 feet long and 65 feet high. Between the legs of the Sphinx is the "Dream Stela" of Thutmose IV that promised Thutmose IV the kingship in return for clearing the sand from around the Sphinx. (See below for a possible connection to the Exodus.)

The third pyramid is that of Menkure, or Mycerinus, standing at a more diminutive height of 203 feet. To the south of this pyramid are three smaller pyramids built for relatives of the pharaoh.

Period of the Exodus *Exodus 12:29–32—Thutmose IV* (1425–1408 BC) followed his father to the throne. Nothing much is known about his reign, although a stela found between the legs of the Sphinx recorded that he dug the Sphinx out of the sand as a youth and so was promised he would someday be king. The "Dream Stela" could be indirect confirmation of the death of Pharaoh's firstborn son at the time of the Exodus since Thutmose IV would not have needed such a promise had he been the firstborn. (The firstborn would have been expected to succeed his father to the throne.)

GOSHEN/CITIES OF THE EXODUS

The "region of Goshen" is the area of Egypt where the Israelites settled (Gen. 46:28–34). It was located on the eastern frontier of Lower Egypt near the route that led up to the "Philistine country" (Ex. 13:17). In Psalm 78:12, 43 this region is called the "region [or pastoral plain] of Zoan"—a city that at that time was located at the mouth of the Bubastic branch of the Nile River. (Today, it is some eighteen miles from the coast.)

Patriarchal Period *Genesis 46:28–47:6*—Jacob led his family to Goshen during the time of the seven-year famine. Joseph asked the pharaoh to give his family permission to dwell in Goshen as shepherds.

Period of the Exodus *Exodus 1:11*—The Israelites living in Goshen were enslaved and forced to build the Egyptian storage cities of Pithom and Rameses.

Exodus 8:22; 9:26—During the plagues on Egypt, God said He would deal differently with "the land of Goshen" so that a number of the plagues affected only the Egyptians and not the Israelites.

Storehouses, like these, were made of sun-dried

KARNAK/THEBES/LUXOR

Karnak is a city with five names. The original Egyptian name for the city was Weset or Newt, which meant simply "the city." During the Middle and New Kingdom periods, the city became the political and religious center for Egypt. The city was also identified with its chief deity, Amun, and became known as No-amon, "the city of Amun," or simply No—"the city." During the Hellenistic period, the Greek name for the city became Thebes, and this is sometimes the name used by Bible translators. Following the Muslim conquest, the magnificent ruins were called in Arabic *al-Qusur*, "the palaces," and this name has come over into English as Luxor.

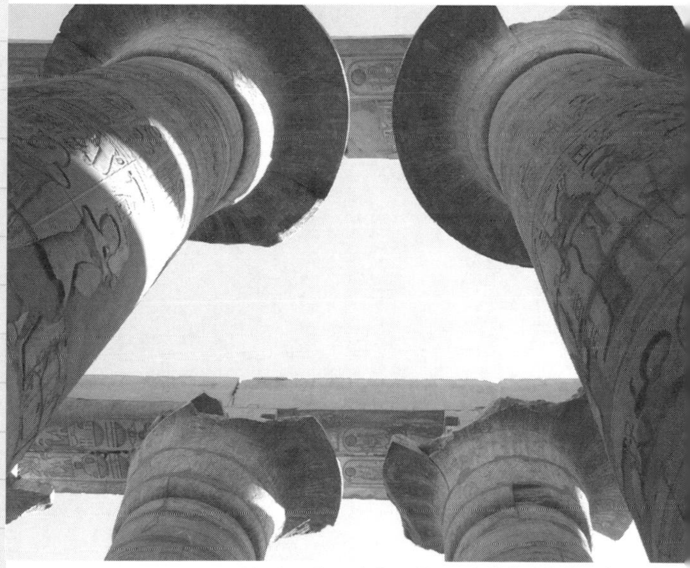

Massive columns in Great Hypostyle Hall of the Karnak temple

Single Kingdom *Nahum 3:8*—Nahum asked Nineveh whether it was "better than Thebes [No-amon]," a city that the Assyrians had attacked and destroyed in 663 BC.

Jeremiah 46:25—God announced that He would punish "Amon god of Thebes" along with the pharaoh and Egypt's false gods.

Ezekiel 30:14–16—Ezekiel announced God's judgment on Thebes and several other cities in Egypt.

Apostolic Age *Hebrews 11:24–26*—Moses would have spent some of his childhood in Pharaoh's house in Thebes. This is certainly one spot where Moses saw the "treasures of Egypt" that the writer of Hebrews says he ultimately rejected.

MEMPHIS

Memphis was founded around 3100 BC by Menes (Narmer), the king who united Upper and Lower Egypt. Memphis allowed Menes to control the land and water routes between Upper Egypt and the Delta. By the Third Dynasty, Memphis had become a sizable city, serving as the administrative and religious center of all Egypt.

Memphis is actually the Greek name for the city; its original name was Ineb-Hedj, "the White Wall"—a name that referred to the white mud-brick wall built around the city by Menes. The Greek name likely came from the transliteration of the name of the pyramid complex of Pepi I at nearby Saqqara, which was called *Mennefer* ("the good place") or, in Coptic, *Menfe*.

Divided Kingdom *Isaiah 19:13*—Isaiah announced God's judgment on Egypt, in part because the princes of Memphis were "deceived."

Hosea 9:6—Hosea predicted that the people of Memphis would be burying those Jews who had fled there for refuge.

Single Kingdom *Jeremiah 2:16*—Jeremiah said the men of Memphis had "shaved the crown of your head," pointing to Judah's humiliating subjection to Egypt.

Jeremiah 44:1—Jeremiah delivered a message to those Jews living Egypt, including those dwelling in Memphis.

Jeremiah 46:14–19—Jeremiah predicted the destruction of Memphis by the Babylonians.

Ezekiel 30:13–16—God threatened to destroy the idols and the leaders in the city of Memphis.

SAQQARA

Saqqara is part of a large necropolis (cemetery) associated with the ancient city of Memphis. The earliest king whose name has been found at Saqqara is Menes/Narmer, the first king of the First Dynasty, who is considered to be the founder of Memphis.

There are fifteen royal pyramids at Saqqara. The earliest Egyptian stone-built pyramid, the Step Pyramid, is also the earliest stone structure in the world. It was built for Djoser, a king of the Third Dynasty (about 2686–2613 BC) by his vizier Imhotep. Nearby is the pyramid of Unas, the last king of the Fifth Dynasty (about 2494–2345 BC). This is the first pyramid to be inscribed with the funerary texts known today as the Pyramid Texts.

Until the construction of these pyramids, mastabas had been the principal form of tomb architecture. A mastaba (Arabic for "bench") is a low rectangular structure built over a shaft that descended to the burial location.

The Step Pyramid of Djoser

SINAI (MOUNT)

Mount Sinai is both the name of a collection of peaks and the biblical name of the peak on which Moses received the Ten Commandments. Jebel Musa is traditionally identified as that peak. The summit of the 7,497-foot mountain can be reached by climbing 3,750 steps hewn out of stone by monks from St. Catherine's Monastery, located just to the north. The summit contains the Chapel of the Holy Trinity, built in 1934 on the site of the original chapel constructed in AD 363.

A view toward the summit of Mount Sinai

St. Catherine's Monastery is located at the foot of Jebel Musa. The monastery was constructed by order of Emperor Justinian and completed in AD 565. It was built atop the supposed location of Moses' burning bush.

Period of the Exodus *Exodus 3:1–2*—Moses was pasturing his father-in-law's flocks at "the mountain of God" when he encountered God in the burning bush.

Exodus 19:1, 18—Three months after leaving Egypt, the Israelites arrived at Mount Sinai, and God's glory came down and rested on the mountain.

Exodus 31:18—God gave Moses the two tablets containing the Law on Mount Sinai.

Divided Kingdom *1 Kings 19:8*—When Elijah fled from Jezebel, he came to Mount Sinai, called Mount Horeb in the text and identified as "the mountain of God."

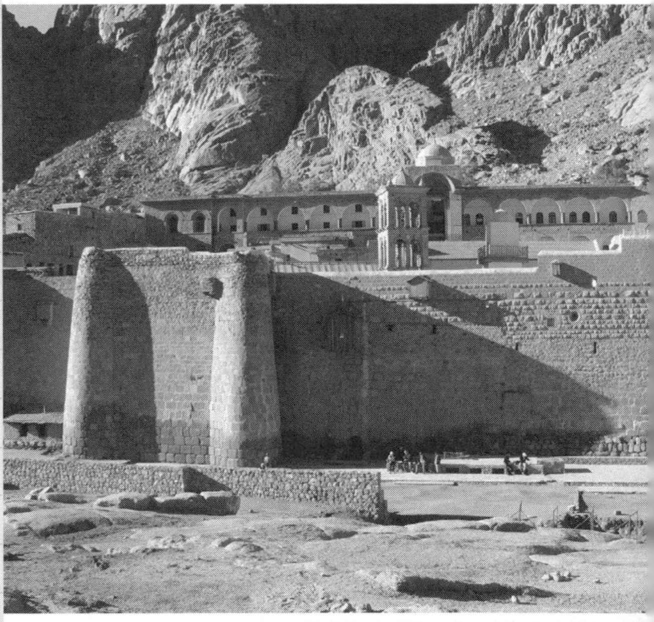

St. Catherine's Monastery at the foot of Mount Si

VALLEY OF THE KINGS/QUEENS

The city of Karnak/Thebes/Luxor was located on the east bank of the Nile River. But the cliffs on the Nile's west bank became the burial ground for the pharaohs. Beginning in the Eighteenth Dynasty and ending in the Twentieth Dynasty, the kings of Egypt abandoned the necropolis at Saqqara and built their tombs in Karnak/Thebes. They abandoned the pyramid-style tombs, choosing instead to cut their tombs into the limestone cliffs.

The Valley of the Kings contains sixty-two known tombs, twenty-four of which were for royal burials. To the southwest of the Valley of the Kings was the Valley of the Queens. Originally this was the burial site for high officials. Later it became the burial site for a number of queens as well as for royal children. The Valley of the Queens contains eighty known tombs built on a smaller scale than those in the Valley of the Kings.

Entrance to the Valley of the Kings

In addition to tombs, the west bank of the Nile also held a number of mortuary temples. The most famous of these is the one built by Queen Hatshepsut at Deir el-Bahri. Another fascinating site is the Colossi of Memnon. These two statues (about sixty-five feet high) represent the deified pharaoh Amenhotep III and once flanked the entrance of the first pylon at his mortuary temple, which is now completely destroyed.

Another site worth visiting is the Ramesseum, a mortuary temple built to worship Rameses II, whose first name was Usermaatre. One feature of the temple was a gigantic statue of Rameses that stood nearly sixty-five feet high. This temple was mentioned by classical writers like Diodorus Siculus who described it in detail as "the tomb of Osymandias" (the Greek transliteration of Usermaatre). Siculus even recorded the inscription on the pedestal of the statue: "King of Kings am I, Osymandias. If anyone would know how great I am and where I lie, let him surpass one of my works" (*Diodorus of Sicily* 47. 167–69). The statue—now lying facedown on the ground—inspired Percy Bysshe Shelley to write his poem "Ozymandias."

Deir el-Bahri, Queen Hatshepsut's mortuary temp

PART FOUR

The Land of Greece

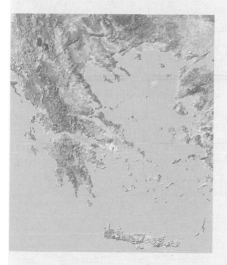

- Let's Go Shopping with Paul
- The Gods of Greece and Rome

LET'S GO SHOPPING WITH PAUL

The center of commerce in most ancient cities was the *agora*, or market area. Although the agora began as an area where people gathered to buy and sell, it eventually became one of the central focal points in most communities. In some cities like Corinth—which was situated on a key international trade route—the agora became a vital part of the region's economy.

The agora was often paved with colonnaded walkways, monuments, sculptures, and other public buildings. Often a *bema*, or speaker's platform, would be erected in the marketplace. The local magistrate would use this location to sit and judge administrative matters. Most of the other buildings in the agora were offices or shops, with the public latrines usually nearby.

The agora of Corinth played a strategic role in the apostle Paul's ministry there. In Acts 18:12–17 the Jews "made a united attack on Paul and brought him into court" (lit., "up to the bema"). Their accusations were rejected, and the synagogue ruler was beaten in front of the bema. When writing to the Corinthians about their worldly actions, Paul reminded the church that "we must all appear before the judgment seat [*bema*] of Christ, that each one may receive what is due him for the things done while in the body, whether good or bad" (2 Cor. 5:10).

The Gods of Greece and Rome

POSITION	GREEK NAME	ROMAN NAME
King of the gods	*Zeus*	*Jupiter*
God of the sun and youth	*Apollo*	*Apollo*
God of war	*Ares*	*Mars*
God of the sea	*Poseidon*	*Neptune*
Messenger of the gods	*Hermes*	*Mercury*
Blacksmith for the gods	*Hephaestus*	*Vulcan*
God of wine and the arts	*Dionysius*	*Bacchus*
God of love	*Eros*	*Cupid*
God of the underworld	*Pluto*	*Pluto*
God of time	*Kronos*	*Saturn*
Queen of the gods	*Hera*	*Juno*
Goddess of agriculture	*Demeter*	*Ceres*
Goddess of the moon, hunting, and fertility	*Artemis*	*Diana*
Goddess of wisdom	*Athena*	*Minerva*
Goddess of love and beauty	*Aphrodite*	*Venus*
Goddess of the home	*Hestia*	*Vesta*
God of health and healing	*Asclepius*	*Asclepius*
Half-god/half-man mythical "hero"	*Heracles*	*Hercules*

Greek Gods in the Book of Acts

"When the crowd saw [the miracle] Paul had done, they shouted in the Lycaonian language, 'The gods have come down to us in human form!' Barnabas they called Zeus, and Paul they called Hermes because he was the chief speaker" (Acts 14:11–12).

"While Paul was waiting for [Silas and Timothy] in Athens, he was greatly distressed to see that the city was full of idols. . . . Paul then stood up in the meeting of the Areopagus and said: 'Men of Athens! I see that in every way you are very religious. For as I walked around and looked carefully at your objects of worship, I even found an altar with this inscription: TO AN UNKNOWN GOD'" (Acts 17:16, 22–23).

"A silversmith named Demetrius, who made silver shrines of Artemis, brought in no little business for the craftsmen. He called them together, along with the workmen in related trades, and said: 'Men, you know we receive a good income from this business. And you see and hear how this fellow Paul has convinced and led astray large numbers of people here in Ephesus and in practically the whole province of Asia. He says that man-made gods are no gods at all. There is danger not only that our trade will lose its good name, but also that the temple of the great goddess Artemis will be discredited, and the goddess herself, who is worshiped throughout the province of Asia and the world, will be robbed of her divine majesty.' When they heard this, they were furious and began shouting: 'Great is Artemis of the Ephesians!'" (Acts 19:24–28).

ATHENS

Athens, the most important city in ancient Greece, was famous for its culture, learning, and great philosophers, including Plato and Aristotle. The city was also renowned for its temples, statues, and monuments. After the Romans conquered Greece, Athens became a *civitas foederata* (a city linked to Rome by treaty), entirely independent of the governor of Achaia and paying no taxes to Rome. Although the Athenians were religious and eager to discuss religion, their spiritual level was not exceptionally high.

The Acropolis and Parthenon from below

Apostolic Age *Acts 17:15–34*—Paul came to Athens on his second missionary journey and preached to the philosophers at the Areopagus (Mars Hill).

1 Thessalonians 3:1–6—While in Athens, Paul sent Timothy back to Thessalonica to see how the new church there was doing, since he had been forced to leave early. Before Timothy could return with news from Thessalonica, Paul left Athens for Corinth (Acts 18:1).

Looking down at the Areopagus (Mars Hill) from the Acro

CORINTH

Corinth was situated at the western end of the narrow isthmus linking central Greece and the Peloponnesian peninsula. Because of its position, Corinth controlled the trade route between northern Greece and the Peloponnesian peninsula as well as the route across the isthmus. Ships would unload cargo and transport it overland for five miles between the eastern port at Cenchrea and the western port at Lechaeum to avoid the

The *bema*, or judgment seat, of Corinth with the Acrocorinth rising majestically in the background

hazardous voyage around the peninsula. The rocky mountain jutting up south of the city, called the Acrocorinth, dominated the landscape around Corinth. In ancient times, a temple to Aphrodite, goddess of love, stood on its crest with one thousand prostitutes serving those who came to "worship." The one thousand prostitutes plus the transient population gave Corinth the reputation of an immoral city. The degree to which Corinth was given over to vice is seen in the coining of the words *korinthiázomi* (lit., "to Corinthianize"), which meant "to practice immorality" and *korinthia kór*, which meant "prostitute."

Apostolic Age *Acts 18:1–18* —On his second missionary journey, Paul came to Corinth after leaving Athens. Paul teamed up for the first time with Aquila and Priscilla in Corinth, and he remained in the city for eighteen months, planting the church. The Jews opposed Paul and brought him before the judgment seat of Gallio, proconsul of Achaia.

1 Corinthians 16:5–9—Paul wrote the letter of 1 Corinthians from Ephesus while on his third missionary journey. Paul wrote to correct a number of problems that had arisen in the Corinthian church after his departure. The letter was written in advance of a planned trip to Corinth by Paul.

Paul made a second, unrecorded visit to Corinth, possibly while he was still at Ephesus (2 Cor. 2:1). The exact nature of the visit is uncertain, but it was not anticipated by Paul when he wrote 1 Corinthians (cf. 1 Cor. 16:5–7). These veiled references imply it was an emergency trip made in haste, possibly to correct some severe problems that had arisen in Corinth.

2 Corinthians 2:1–4; 12–13—Paul wrote the letter of 2 Corinthians from Macedonia (possibly Philippi) when he received good news from Titus about the repentance in the church at Corinth. Paul was coming to

Corinth to complete the collection being made for the saints in Jerusalem (2 Cor. 9:1–5). This was to be his third trip to Corinth (12:14; 13:1–2).

Acts 20:2–3—Paul went to Greece to complete the collection for the saints and spent three months in Greece (some of which, no doubt, was spent in Corinth).

Remains of the temple of Apollo

CRETE

Crete is a large island in the Mediterranean Sea that forms the southern boundary of the Aegean Sea. The island is 156 miles long and varies in width from 8 to 35 miles. The mountains in the interior reach a height of 8,000 feet. These drop sharply into the Mediterranean Sea along the southern coast. As a result, most of Crete's good harbors are on the northern side. During the Bronze Age (ca. 2000–1200 BC), the Minoan civilization flourished on Crete. The capital was at Knossos, and extensive ruins of the Minoan palace at Knossos can still be seen. In the Old Testament, the island of Crete is referred to as Caphtor, and the people who came from Crete are called "Caphtorim," "Caphtorites," "Cherethites," and "Kerethites." They are either identical to, or closely related to, the Philistines. The inhabitants of Crete were not known for their strong moral integrity. In Greek literature, "to Cretanize" meant "to lie."

Period of the Exodus *Deuteronomy 2:23*—Moses used the inhabitants of Crete (who, possibly, became the Philistines) as an example of those who drove out other inhabitants and settled in their land. "And as for the Avvites who lived in villages as far as Gaza, the Caphtorites coming out from Caphtor destroyed them and settled in their place."

United Kingdom *1 Samuel 30:14*—The land of the Kerethites was raided by the same group who destroyed David's city of Ziklag. The land of the Kerethites was the southern Gaza strip area and was also considered the land of the Philistines.

2 Samuel 8:18; 15:18; 20:7, 23—Part of David's personal contingent of soldiers and bodyguards included "Kerethites and Pelethites." These were a special military contingent of mercenary soldiers who had their own leader. "Joab was over Israel's entire army; Benaiah son of Jehoiada was over the Kerethites and Pelethites" (2 Sam. 20:23).

Divided Kingdom *Amos 9:7*—Amos explained the origin of the Philistines: "Did I [the Lord] not bring Israel up from Egypt, the Philistines from Caphtor and the Arameans from Kir?"

Single Kingdom *Ezekiel 25:16*—Ezekiel predicted God's destruction of the Philistines/Kerethites because of their persecution of Israel. "I am about to stretch out my hand against the Philistines, and I will cut off the Kerethites and destroy those remaining along the coast."

After naming the cities of Gaza, Ashkelon, Ashdod, and Ekron—four of the five cities that were part of the land of the Philistines—Zephaniah predicted God's destruction of the Philistines/Kerethites: "Woe to you who live by the sea, O Kerethite people; the word of the LORD is against you, O Canaan, land of the Philistines" (Zeph. 2:5).

Apostolic Age *Acts 2:11*—Jews from Crete were present in Jerusalem on the Day of Pentecost.

Acts 27:7–15, 21—On his way to Rome as a prisoner, Paul's ship "sailed to the lee of

Crete, opposite Salmone." The book of Acts describes the ship's journey along the southern coast to a place called Fair Havens, near the town of Lasea, a harbor "unsuitable to winter in" (27:12). Trying to reach Crete, "the ship was caught by [a] storm" with hurricane-force winds (v. 15).

Titus 1:5, 12–13—After his first imprisonment, Paul evidently returned to Crete to continue his missionary activity. Paul journeyed on but left Titus in Crete to finish the work he had begun. Paul quoted Epimenides (a sixth-century BC native of Knossos, Crete) who wrote that "Cretans are always liars, evil brutes, lazy gluttons." Sadly, Paul noted, "This testimony is true" (Titus 1:12–13).

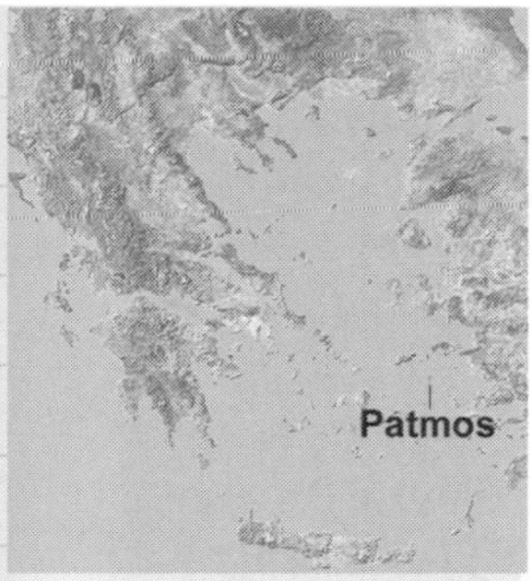

PATMOS

Patmos is located at the northwestern end of a group of islands known as the Dodecanese. The island is of volcanic origin and has a rugged coastline. An isthmus only a few hundred yards wide, on which the island's harbor lies, separates the northern end of the island from the southern half.

Patmos was one of the many places to which Rome banished exiles. According to Irenaeus and

Looking down at the harbor of Patmos and the narrow isthmus that divides the island in two

Eusebius, the apostle John was banished from Ephesus to Patmos in the fourteenth year of the reign of Domitian (AD 95). He remained there for a year until after Domitian's death in AD 96, when he is said to have returned to Ephesus.

Apostolic Age *Revelation 1:9–11*—Revelation was written by the apostle John while he was exiled on Patmos because of his faith.

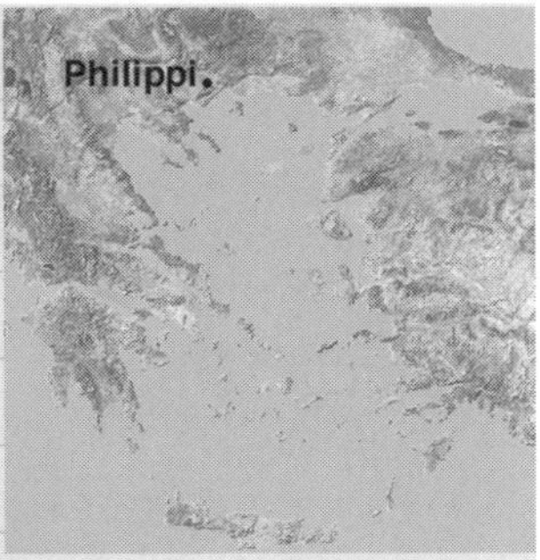

PHILIPPI

Philippi was a Roman colony and the leading city in the district of Macedonia. The city was located at the eastern end of the Egnatian Way (via Egnatia), which was a major east–west route across Greece.

Gold was discovered on Mount Pangaeum, and settlers from the island of Thassos seized the area from the local Greeks and Thracians. They founded a city near the site of Philippi and called it Krenides ("spring" in Greek) because of the spring-fed river. Philip II of Macedon, the father of Alexander the Great, saw the strategic importance of Krenides and captured it. He rebuilt the city and renamed it after himself, Philippi. In 168 BC the area passed into Roman hands. The gold supply eventually was exhausted, and the city declined in importance.

However, Philippi again became important because on its plains the future of the Roman republic was decided. In 42 BC Octavius (later called Augustus Caesar) and Mark Antony fought and defeated Brutus and Cassius (the assassins of Julius Caesar). In honor of the victory, Philippi was made a Roman colony, and many of the Roman legionnaires settled there. The city was given the right to the Law of Italy (*ius Italicum*) along with many of the privileges and immunities of Italy—especially immunity from taxation.

Apostolic Age *Acts 16:11–40*—Philippi was the first European city in which Paul preached. Lydia, a merchant from Thyatira, became the first convert in Europe. Paul healed a slave girl who was possessed with a spirit of divination, and her owners had Paul and Silas beaten and placed in prison. The

The agora, or marketplace, of ancient Philippi

Philippian jailer became a believer after an earthquake occurred in the night. Paul and Silas were released, and they left Philippi to continue their journey.

2 Corinthians 8:1–5; Philippians 1:1–11—In spite of severe poverty and great difficulties, the congregation at Philippi supported Paul's ministry and remained close to him.

Philippians 1:13–14—Paul wrote his letter to the Philippians while under house arrest in Rome. He wrote to encourage them to remain faithful and joyful, to thank them for their generous gift to him, and to report on his current circumstances.

PART FIVE

The Land of Jordan

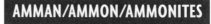

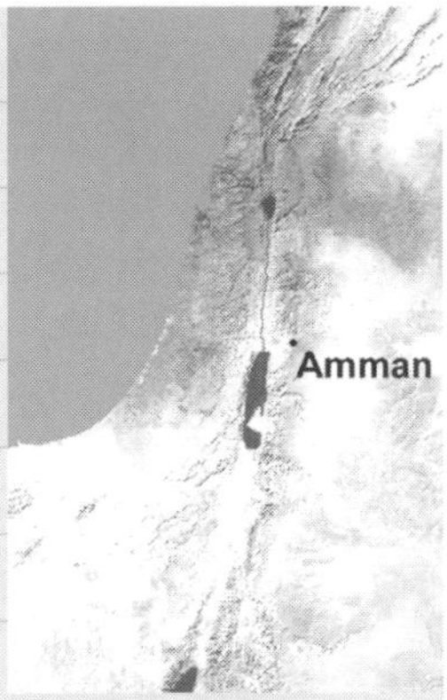

AMMAN/AMMON/AMMONITES

The Ammonites descended from a son born to Lot by his youngest daughter following the destruction of Sodom and Gomorrah (Gen. 19:30–38). Because the Ammonites descended from Lot (Abraham's nephew), they were considered a "related" nation to Israel. "When you come to the Ammonites, do not harass them or provoke them to war, for I will not give you possession of any land belonging to the Ammonites. I have given it as a possession to the descendants of Lot" (Deut. 2:19). The Ammonites occupied the tableland east of the Jordan Valley that stretched into the Arabian Desert. Their northern boundary extended to the Jabbok River, while their southern boundary was the Arnon River. The capital of the Ammonites was Rabbah (sometimes called Rabbath-ammon). The national god of the Ammonites was Molech.

By New Testament times, the city of Rabbah had become the southernmost city in the league of cities called the Decapolis. Its name had been changed to Philadelphia (not to be confused with the Philadelphia in Asia Minor named in Revelation). Today, ancient Rabbah is the modern city of Amman, Jordan, the capital of the Hashemite Kingdom of Jordan.

Patriarchal Period *Genesis 19:30–38*—At her sister's urging, Lot's younger daughter got her father drunk and had sexual relations with him. The child born of that union was named Ben-Ammi ("son of my father"), and the Ammonites descended from him.

Period of the Exodus *Deuteronomy 2:19–21, 37*—God prohibited Israel from taking the land of the Ammonites.

Period of the Judges *Judges 3:13*—The Ammonites united with Eglon, king of Moab, to oppress Israel and control the city of Jericho.

Judges 10–11—The Ammonites oppressed Israel until Jephthah rose as a judge to deliver the Israelites from them.

United Kingdom *1 Samuel 11*—Saul's first act as king was to rescue the people of Jabesh Gilead from an Ammonite attack.

2 Samuel 10:1–14; 1 Chronicles 19:1–15—The Ammonites humiliated a delegation sent by King David and brought about war with Israel. Joab defeated the Ammonites in battle near Medeba.

2 Samuel 11—Joab and the men of Israel fought the Ammonites and besieged their capital of Rabbah. David remained in Jerusalem and committed adultery with Bathsheba. Uriah, Bathsheba's husband, was killed in the siege of Rabbah.

Divided Kingdom *2 Chronicles 20:1–24*—The Ammonites, Moabites, and Edomites united and crossed the Dead Sea at the tongue of land called the Lisan to attack Judah. Jehoshaphat led the Israelites into the wilderness, only to discover that God had already intervened and caused the allies to fight among themselves and kill one another.

2 Chronicles 26:8; 27:5—King Uzziah forced the Ammonites to pay tribute to him. Following Uzziah's death, King Jotham attacked and defeated the Ammonites, forcing them to continue paying tribute to Judah.

Amos 1:13–15—God condemned the

Ammonites for attacking the Israelite land of Gilead, east of the Sea of Galilee.

Babylonian Captivity *Jeremiah 40:13–14; 41:2–15*—After Jerusalem's fall to the Babylonians, the king of Ammon sent Ishmael to assassinate Gedaliah, the governor of Judah appointed by the Babylonians. After the assassination, Ishmael fled to Ammon.

Jeremiah 49:1–6—Jeremiah predicted the imminent destruction of "Rabbah of the Ammonites." But he also predicted the Ammonites' eventual restoration.

Ezekiel 21:18–27—When Nebuchadnezzar brought his army from Babylon, he had to decide whether to attack first Rabbah of the Ammonites or Jerusalem. Ezekiel prophesied God would direct Nebuchadnezzar to Jerusalem.

Ezekiel 25:1–7—Ezekiel predicted the imminent destruction of the Ammonites because they rejoiced when the Babylonians destroyed Jerusalem.

Daniel 11:41—Daniel predicted that Edom, Moab, and Ammon would not fall into the hands of the final world ruler who would invade Israel just before the coming of Israel's Messiah.

Restoration *Ezra 9:1; Nehemiah 4:7; 13:23*—The Ammonites harassed the Jews who returned from captivity, threatened the security of those who were rebuilding Jerusalem, and tried to corrupt the remnant through intermarriage.

ARNON RIVER

The Arnon River runs from east to west and drains into the Dead Sea approximately halfway down its eastern side. From antiquity, it has served as a natural barrier and border.

Period of the Exodus "The Arnon is the border of Moab, between Moab and the Amorites" (Num. 21:13).

King Balak of Moab went to meet the prophet Balaam at a "Moabite town on the Arnon border" (Num. 22:36).

Deuteronomy 2:24–37; Joshua 12:1–2—Israel captured all the land of Sihon, king of the Amorites, which began at "Aroer on the rim of the Arnon Gorge" (Deut. 2:36).

Deuteronomy 3:8—The territory of the Amorites, captured by Israel, extended from the Arnon Gorge north to Mount Hermon.

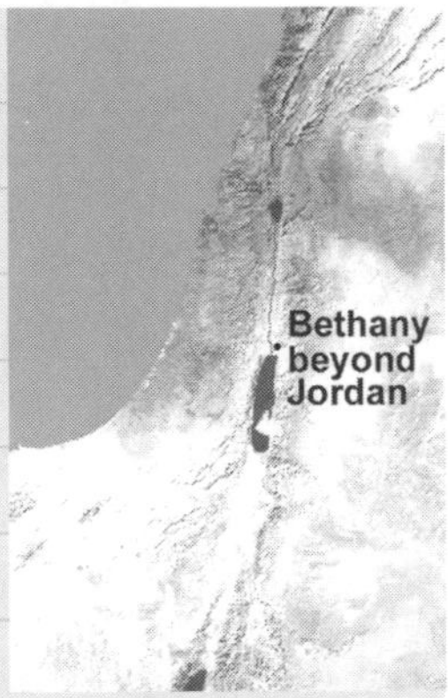

BETHANY BEYOND THE JORDAN/PLAINS OF MOAB

On the eastern bank of the Jordan River is "Bethany beyond the Jordan," an important place associated with the lives of Jesus and John the Baptist. This is also the place where the twelve tribes of Israel camped just prior to entering the Promised Land. A small natural hill in the area is called *Tell Mar Elias*, or "Elijah's Hill," identifying it as the place from which Elijah ascended to heaven.

A new church marks the traditional spot of Bethany where Jesus baptized in the Jordan River by John the Bap

Period of the Exodus The Israelites arrived at the plains of Moab "along the Jordan across from Jericho" (Num. 22:1).

Numbers 26; Deuteronomy 1:5—Moses numbered the sons of Israel on the plains of

Moab and delivered his last messages (found in the book of Deuteronomy) here.

Deuteronomy 34:8—After the death of Moses, the nation of Israel mourned his death for thirty days on the plains of Moab.

Joshua 13:8–32—Moses allotted territory to Reuben, Gad, and half the tribe of Manasseh while they were camped on the plains of Moab.

Divided Kingdom *2 Kings 2:1–15*—Elijah and Elisha crossed the Jordan near Jericho, and Elisha watched as God took Elijah to heaven in a chariot of fire.

Life of Christ *John 1:28–29*—Jesus was baptized by John while he was baptizing at "Bethany on the other side of the Jordan."

John 10:40; 11:1–18—Jesus "went back across the Jordan, to the place where John had been baptizing in the early days" (John 10:40) after He had been threatened with stoning in Jerusalem. Jesus went from here to the other Bethany near Jerusalem to raise Lazarus from the dead.

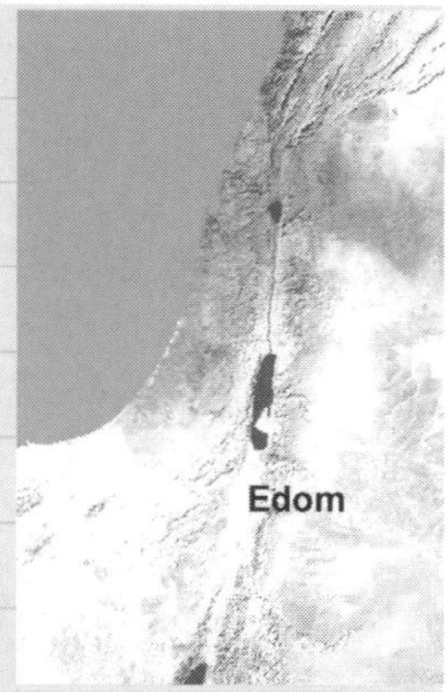

EDOM/EDOMITES

The Edomites were the descendants of Jacob's twin brother, Esau (Gen. 25:21–26; 36:9). The name Edom comes from the word meaning "red," and it described Esau's physical characteristics at birth (25:25). It also became his nickname because of his fondness for red lentil stew, the "red stuff" for which he bartered away his birthright (vv. 30–31 NASB). Finally, the name is an apt description of the land occupied by the Edomites with its red sandstone rock.

Because the Edomites descended from Jacob's brother, they were considered a "brother" nation to Israel. Moses commanded Israel, "Do not abhor an Edomite, for he is your brother" (Deut. 23:7).

The northern border of the land of Edom was the Wadi Zered, which flows from east to west and joins the Arabah at the southeastern tip of the Dead Sea. The land of the Edomites extended south to the Red Sea, or Gulf of Aqaba.

Patriarchal Period *Genesis 32:3; 36:6–8*—Esau left the land of Canaan and settled in the land of Seir, later known as Edom.

Period of the Exodus *Numbers 20:14–21*—The Edomites refused to let Israel pass through their land as the Israelites made their way up the east side of the Dead Sea. Israel had asked for permission to travel on the "king's highway" (the main north–south road from Damascus to the Gulf of Aqaba) where it passed through Edom.

Numbers 34:3; Joshua 15:1—The Wilderness of Zin, along the southeastern border of the tribe of Judah, was the boundary between Israel and Edom.

United Kingdom *1 Samuel 21:7; 22:9–19*—Doeg the Edomite spotted David when he fled from Saul to the priests of Nob to retrieve Goliath's sword. Doeg later reported the event to Saul and personally killed eighty-five priests at the order of Saul.

2 Samuel 8:13–14; 1 Chronicles 18:12–13—David destroyed an Edomite army and conquered the land of Edom.

1 Kings 9:26; 11:14; 2 Chronicles 8:17—Solomon built a fleet of ships at Ezion Geber near Elath "in Edom, on the shore of the Red Sea." God raised up Hadad the Edomite as an adversary to judge Solomon for his unfaithfulness.

Divided Kingdom *2 Kings 3:4–27*—The kings of Judah, Israel, and Edom led their armies through the Desert of Edom in a surprise attack against the king of Moab.

2 Kings 14:7; 16:6—King Amaziah of Judah defeated ten thousand Edomites in a major battle and captured the city of Sela. Later the king of Aram captured Elath from Judah, and drove out the people of Judah. The Edomites moved back to populate the city.

2 Chronicles 20—The Ammonites, Moabites, and Edomites united and crossed the Dead Sea at the tongue of land called the Lisan to attack Judah. Jehoshaphat led the Israelites into the wilderness, only to discover that God had already intervened and caused the allies to fight among themselves and kill one another.

2 Chronicles 28:17—The Edomites attacked Judah during the reign of Ahaz.

Isaiah 11:14—Isaiah prophesied a day when God's people would triumph over Edom, Moab, and Ammon.

Isaiah 34:1–11; 63:1–3—In picturing God's final judgment on the earth as He intervened to judge sin and restore His people Israel, Isaiah recorded that God's sword "descends in judgment on Edom" (34:5). The prophet pictured God coming from Edom with His robe stained in the blood of His enemies.

Joel 3:19; Amos 1:11–12—God would make Edom a desolate waste because of their violence against the people of Judah. Through Amos, God condemned Edom for pursuing "his brother [Judah] with a sword, stifling all compassion" (Amos 1:11).

The Book of Obadiah—The prophet Obadiah described God's judgment on the prideful people of Edom.

Babylonian Captivity *Psalm 137:7*—The psalmist asked God to judge the Edomites for their boastful taunting over Jerusalem when it fell to the Babylonians.

Jeremiah 49:7–22—Jeremiah described God's judgment against Edom.

Lamentations 4:21–22—Edom rejoiced over the fall of Jerusalem, but God promised to punish Edom for their sin.

Ezekiel 25:12–14; 35:1–15—God vowed to destroy Edom because the Edomites had taken revenge on the people of Judah and because the Edomites tried to take by force the land God had promised to His people Israel.

Daniel 11:41—Daniel predicted that Edom, Moab, and Ammon would not fall into the hands of the final world ruler who would invade Israel just before the coming of Israel's Messiah.

Restoration *Malachi 1:4*—God vowed the Edomites would not be allowed to rise again. Instead they would remain under the wrath of the Lord.

JABBOK RIVER

The Jabbok River runs from east to west and drains into the Jordan River approximately halfway between the Sea of Galilee and the Dead Sea. From antiquity, it has served as a natural barrier and border dividing Upper Gilead from Lower Gilead.

Patriarchal Period *Genesis 32*—Jacob wrestled with God at Peniel by the Jabbok River when he returned to the Promised Land after his years in Paddan Aram. It was here that God renamed Jacob and called him "Israel."

Period of Conquest *Deuteronomy 3:16*—The Jabbok River was the boundary between the Israelites on the east of the Jordan River and the Ammonites.

Period of the Judges *Judges 11:13–33*—The Ammonites had lost some of their land to the Amorites before the time of the Exodus. Their desire to retake that land from the Israelites (who had captured it from Sihon, king of the Amorites) led to Ammon's defeat at the hands of Jephthah and the Israelites.

View down the Jabbok River

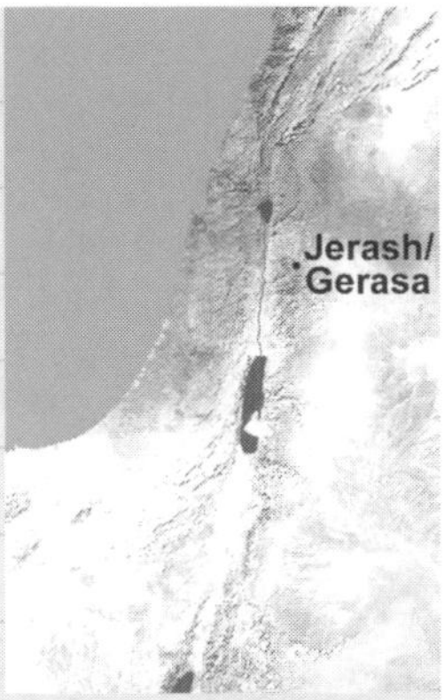

JERASH/GERASA

The modern city of Jerash in Jordan preserves the name of the ancient city of Gerasa, one of the most important cities in the region of the Decapolis. The city is located about twenty-five miles north of Amman and about forty miles southeast of the Sea of Galilee. Jerash has some of the best-preserved Roman ruins in the Middle East.

The only possible reference to Gerasa in the New Testament occurs in the account of Jesus casting the demons into the herd of swine. Matthew 8:28–34 records the exact location

The agora of Jerash (ancient Ge

where the miracle occurred. Matthew, writing to a Jewish audience more familiar with the geographical details of the land, could record the specific village along the shore of the Sea of Galilee. However, Mark (writing to a Roman

The theater of Jerash

audience) and Luke (writing to a Greek audience) recorded the nearest large city that would be familiar to their readers. While there is a textual problem that divides scholars, the two possible cities named by Mark and Luke are Gadara (a smaller city six miles from the Sea of Galilee) or Gerasa (the larger city forty miles from the Sea of Galilee). If Gerasa is the correct textual reading, then Mark and Luke were pointing to the region dominated by the city called Gerasa (modern Jerash).

Life of Christ Jesus and His disciples crossed the Sea of Galilee "to the region of the Gerasenes [i.e., Gerasa]" (Mark 5:1).

Jesus and His disciples "sailed to the region of the Gerasenes [i.e., Gerasa], which is across the lake from Galilee" (Luke 8:26).

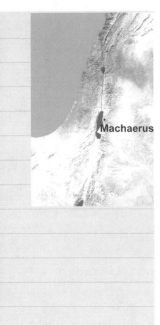

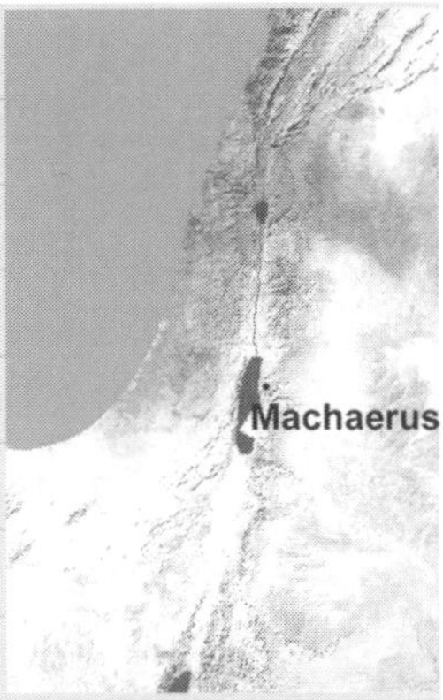

MACHAERUS

The dramatic hilltop palace/fortress of Machaerus, known today as Mukawir, is the place where John the Baptist was beheaded. The site is located twelve miles southwest of modern-day Madaba on a promontory overlooking the Dead Sea. It is protected on three sides by deep ravines.

A fortress was first built at Machaerus by the Hasmonean ruler Alexander Jannaeus (103–76 BC) to defend the region of Perea against the expansionist Nabateans. His widow, Alexandra, confident of the site's security, stored her treasure here. The Romans destroyed it in 63 BC. It was eventually restored by Herod the Great (37–4 BC) who, according to the Jewish historian Josephus, "built a wall round the very summit and erected towers at the corners. . . . In the middle of this enclosure he built a palace, breath-taking in size and beauty."

Life of Christ *Matthew 14:1–12; cf. Mark 6:14–29*—When Herod Antipas divorced his Nabatean wife to marry Herodias, his brother Philip's wife, John the Baptist publicly condemned his behavior. Herod Antipas imprisoned John at Machaerus, and it was here that Herodias's daughter Salome danced and demanded John's head on a platter.

The well-pro hilltop fortr Machaerus w spot where J the Baptist w beheaded.

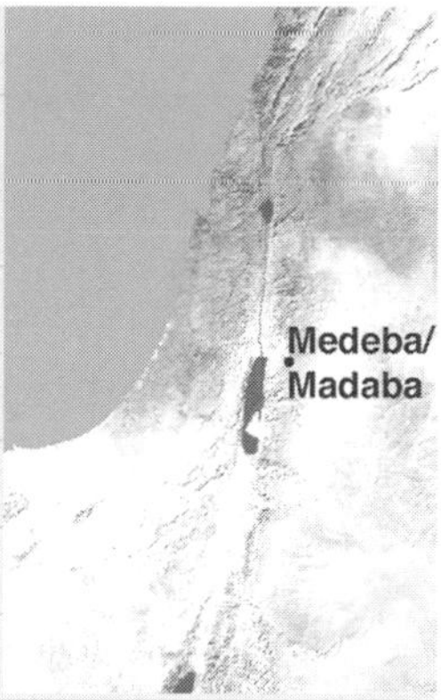

MEDEBA/MADABA

The Medeba of the Bible is today the Arabic town of Madaba. Also known as "the City of Mosaics," the town is famous for its spectacular Byzantine-era mosaics, which are scattered throughout the town's homes and churches. Located on the king's highway just nineteen miles south of Amman, Madaba is best known for the sixth-century mosaic map of the Holy Land, in which Jerusalem and its surrounding regions are depicted.

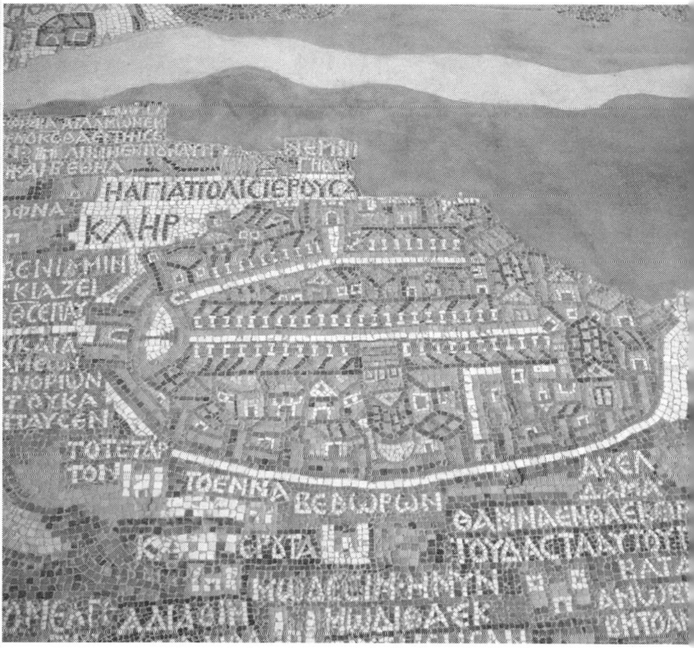

An ancient mosaic in the floor of a church in modern Madaba pictures Jerusalem as it looked in the Byzantine era.

Period of the Exodus *Numbers 21:21–25, 30–31*—Israel defeated Sihon king of the Amorites and captured his territory, including Medeba.

Joshua 13:15–16—The tribe of Reuben received "the whole plateau past Medeba" as part of its inheritance.

Divided Kingdom *Isaiah 15:2*—Isaiah predicted the inhabitants of Moab would weep over the destruction of Nebo and Medeba.

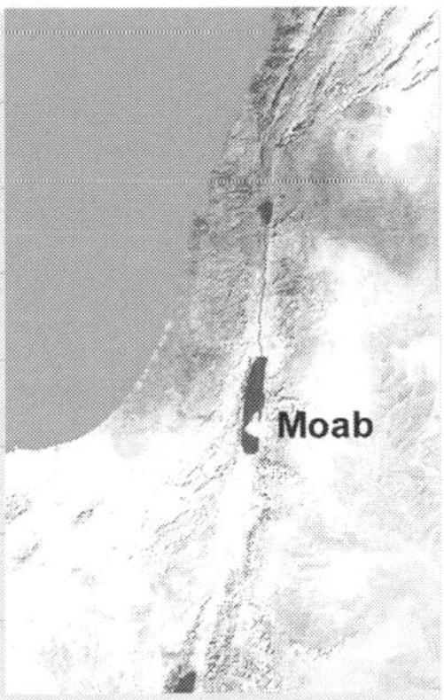

MOAB/MOABITES

The Moabites descended from a son born to Lot and his oldest daughter following the destruction of Sodom and Gomorrah (Gen. 19:30–38). Because the Moabites descended from Lot (Abraham's nephew), they were considered a "related" nation to Israel. "Do not harass the Moabites or provoke them to war, for I will not give you any part of their land. I have given Ar to the descendants of Lot as a possession" (Deut. 2:9). The Moabites occupied the tableland east of the Dead Sea. Their northern boundary extended to the Arnon River, and their southern boundary extended to the Zered River. However, in times of strength their territory did expand northward beyond the Arnon River. Thus, the place where Israel crossed the Jordan into the Promised Land was called the "plains of Moab." The national god of the Moabites was Chemosh.

Patriarchal Period *Genesis 19:30–38*—Lot's oldest daughter got her father drunk and had sexual relations with him. The child born of that union was named Moab, and the Moabites descended from him.

Period of the Exodus *Numbers 21:11–13; Judges 11:17–18*—Israel skirted past Moab on its journey northward along the eastern side of the Dead Sea.

Numbers 22–25; Revelation 2:14—Balak, king of Moab, summoned the prophet Balaam to curse the nation of Israel. Although Balaam was unable to curse Israel outright, he evidently urged the Moabite women to entice the men of Israel into idolatry.

Deuteronomy 2:9–18—God prohibited Israel from taking the land of the Moabites.

Period of the Judges *Judges 3:12–30*—Eglon, king of Moab, oppressed Israel for eighteen years and controlled the city of Jericho until he was defeated by the judge Ehud.

The Book of Ruth—Elimelech, Naomi, and their two sons fled to Moab to escape a famine in Bethlehem. Naomi's husband and two sons died. She returned to Bethlehem accompanied by one of her daughters-in-law, Ruth the Moabitess. Ruth married Boaz, and from their line came King David (Ruth 4:22) and Jesus (Matt. 1:5, 16).

United Kingdom *1 Samuel 14:47*—King Saul conducted military campaigns against Moab.

1 Samuel 22:3–4—David, while a fugitive from Saul, took his parents to live in Moab.

2 Samuel 8:2; 1 Chronicles 18:2—David conquered the Moabites and made them his subjects.

Divided Kingdom *2 Kings 1:1*—After King Ahab's death, Moab rebelled against the northern kingdom of Israel.

2 Kings 3—The kings of Israel, Judah, and Edom attacked and defeated the Moabites.

2 Chronicles 20—The Ammonites, Moabites, and Edomites united together and crossed the Dead Sea at the Lisan to attack Judah. God would intervene and cause the allies to fight among themselves and kill one another.

Isaiah 11:14;15–16—Isaiah prophesied of a day when God's people would triumph over

Edom, Moab, and Ammon and presented God's oracle of judgment against the people of Moab because of their excessive pride.

Amos 2:1–3—Amos announced God's judgment on the people of Moab because of their callous disregard even for the dead.

Babylonian Captivity *Jeremiah 48*—Jeremiah presented God's prophecy of destruction against the people of Moab for their prideful self–reliance and their gloating over Judah's destruction.

Ezekiel 25:8–11—Ezekiel predicted Moab's destruction because of the nation's refusal to acknowledge God's special place for Israel.

Daniel 11:41—Daniel predicted that Edom, Moab, and Ammon would not fall into the hands of the final world ruler who would invade Israel just before the coming of Israel's Messiah.

Restoration *Nehemiah 13:23–27*—Nehemiah rebuked the people of Judah for mixed marriages, including marriages to women of Moab.

NABATEANS

The Nabateans were Semitic nomads who developed and controlled the land caravan routes in the Middle East. Their early history is obscure, but by the fourth century BC they had taken control of Petra from the Edomites, forcing the remaining Edomite population to migrate westward into the Negev and wilderness area in southern Judea.

Although the Nabateans began as nomadic traders, they eventually settled into cities that sat strategically along the main trade routes. Several such cities are in Israel (Mampsis/Mamshit, Avdat/Oboda), but the most well-known city is Petra in Jordan. The beautiful buildings carved into the hillside were constructed by the Nabateans and, later, by the Romans who captured the city in AD 106.

The Nabateans' sudden, swift conquest of the land of Edom and expulsion of the Edomites seems to confirm Obadiah's prophecy against Edom. "All your allies will force you to the border; your friends will deceive and overpower you; those who eat your bread will set a trap for you, but you will not detect it" (Obadiah 7). The Edomites welcomed the caravans of the Nabateans, and the wealth they brought, into their land . . . only to discover their "allies" would later become their conquerors.

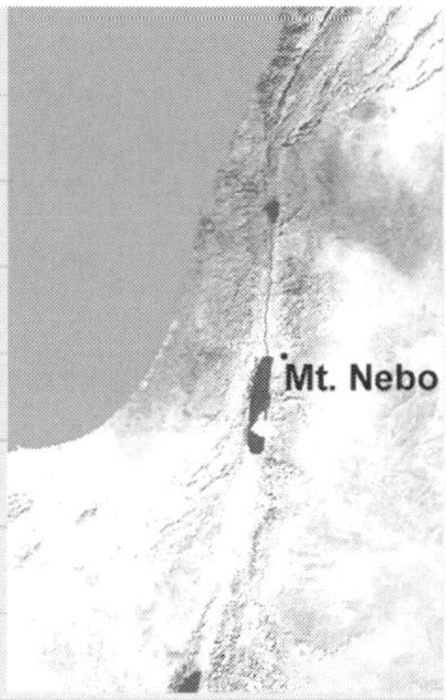

NEBO (MOUNT)

Mount Nebo, also identified with Pisgah, was located northeast of the Dead Sea overlooking the Jordan Valley opposite Jericho. A town with the same name was nearby. It is unclear whether the town was named for the mountain or the mountain named for the town.

Period of the Exodus *Numbers 23:13–14*—The king of Moab took Balaam the prophet to "the top of Pisgah" in an effort to get Balaam to curse Israel.

Numbers 32:1–3, 37–38—The tribe of Reuben received the city of Nebo as part of their tribal inheritance.

Deuteronomy 32:49; 34:1—God allowed Moses to view the Promised Land from "Mount Nebo in Moab, across from Jericho." The specific mountain on which Moses stood was called "the top of Pisgah."

Divided Kingdom *Isaiah 15:2*—Isaiah predicted the inhabitants of Moab would weep over the destruction of Nebo and Medeba.

Single Kingdom *Jeremiah 48:1, 21–22*—Jeremiah predicted the destruction of Nebo and the other cities located on the "plateau."

View of the Dead Sea and the Jordan Valley from Mount Nebo

PETRA

Petra, the rose-red capital of the Nabateans, was originally a city of the Edomites (2 Kings 14:7). Some believe the Old Testament city of Sela (from the Hebrew word meaning "jagged cliff, craggy rock") is the same as the Nabatean city of Petra (from the Greek word meaning "the rock"). The city of Petra is located in a semi-landlocked valley on the eastern side of the Arabah, approximately fifty miles south of the Dead Sea.

The normal entrance into the city of Petra is through the Siq ("cleft"), a winding fissure in the eastern ridge. At the end of the Siq, the path

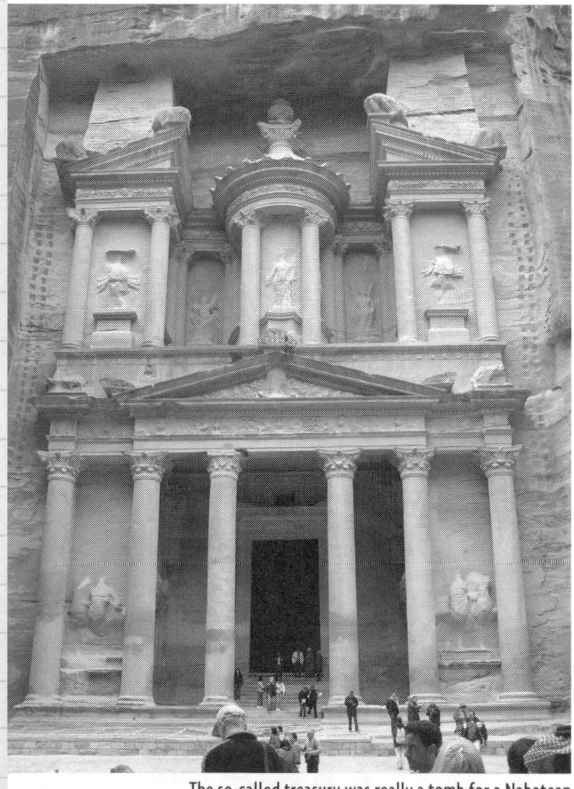

The so-called treasury was really a tomb for a Nabatean king that was carved into the face of the rock.

opens up to a canyon . . . and a spectacular view of a temple carved into the face of the rock.

Some Bible teachers believe the people of Israel will flee to Petra during the period of tribulation immediately preceding the return of Jesus Christ to earth to set up His kingdom. These teachers cite several passages of Scripture to support their view. Those Scriptures are listed below.

Divided Kingdom "All the stars of the heavens will be dissolved and the sky rolled up like a scroll; all the starry host will fall like withered leaves from the vine, like shriveled figs from the fig tree. My sword . . . descends in judgment on Edom, the people I have totally destroyed. The sword of the LORD is bathed in blood" (Isa. 34:4–6).

"Who is this coming from Edom, from Bozrah, with his garments stained crimson? Who is this, robed in splendor, striding forward in the greatness of his strength? 'It is I, speaking in righteousness, mighty to save'" (Isa. 63:1).

Life of Christ "So when you see standing in the holy place 'the abomination that causes desolation,' spoken of through the prophet Daniel—let the reader understand— then let those who are in Judea flee to the mountains" (Matt. 24:15–16).

Apostolic Age "The woman fled into the desert to a place prepared for her by God, where she might be taken care of for 1,260 days" (Rev. 12:6).

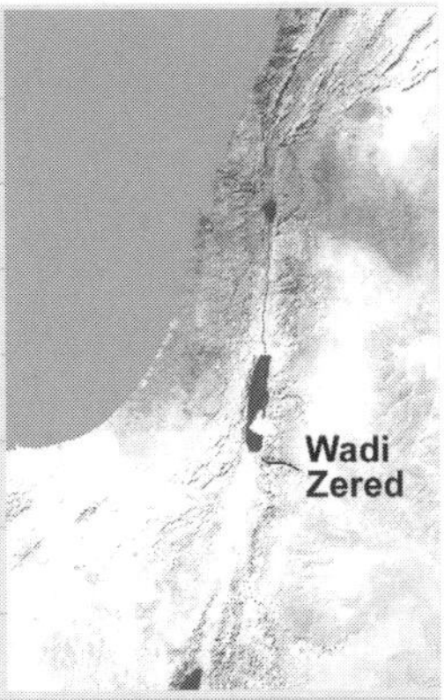

WADI ZERED

The Wadi Zered runs from southeast to northwest and drains into the southern edge of the Dead Sea. From antiquity, it has served as a natural barrier and border. It was the traditional border between Moab and Edom.

Period of the Exodus *Numbers 21:12; Deuteronomy 2:13–14*—Israel camped by the Wadi Zered on their journey around the eastern side of the Dead Sea.

Divided Kingdom *2 Kings 3:16–27*—The valley that filled with water when Israel, Judah, and Edom attacked Moab was probably the Wadi Zered on Moab's border.

Isaiah 15:7—The "Ravine of the Poplars" over which Moab's wealth would be carried is probably the Wadi Zered.

Amos 6:14—The "valley of the Arabah" named by Amos was probably the Wadi Zered, and it marked the southernmost boundary controlled by the king of Israel.

PART SIX

The Land of Turkey

- A Brief Guide to the History of Asia Minor
- The Seven Churches of Revelation 2–3

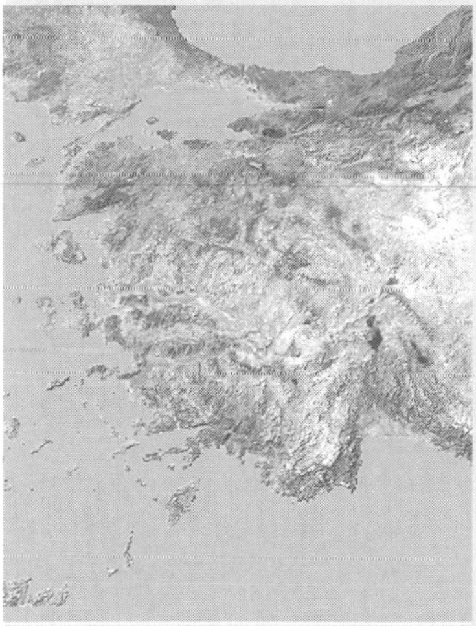

A BRIEF GUIDE TO THE HISTORY OF ASIA MINOR

The Persian Period

By capturing the city of Sardis in 547 BC and defeating the Lydians in 546 BC, the Persians gained control of all Asia Minor—modern-day Turkey—which they dominated for the next two hundred years.

In 490 BC Darius the Great launched an attack against the Greek mainland, but the Greeks defeated his army at the Battle of Marathon. Darius's son, Xerxes, led the Persian army westward in another attempt to conquer Greece in 480 BC. After a delay at Thermopylae, the Persian army captured and sacked Athens. However, the Persian fleet was destroyed by the Greeks at the Battle of Salamis. Xerxes was forced to abandon his conquest of Greece, but the Persians continued to control Asia Minor.

The Hellenistic Period

The Hellenistic period began with Alexander the Great, who was born in 356 BC. Alexander's father, Philip II of Macedonia, united all the Greek city-states except Sparta and conquered Thrace.

At age twenty, Alexander became king when his father died. Over the next thirteen years he expanded his empire east to Iran and India and south to Egypt and North Africa. Alexander began his conquests in 333 BC when he and his army crossed the Hellespont and entered Asia Minor. He fought with the Persians at the Granicus River, and his smaller army routed the larger Persian force.

That fall, Darius III mustered a large army to attack Alexander. However, Alexander marched across Asia Minor and through the Cilician gates near the city of Tarsus (the hometown of the apostle Paul). Alexander's forces fought Darius's army on the narrow Plain of Issus, and the Greeks killed 110,000 Persian soldiers and captured Darius's wife and family.

During the next year Alexander moved his forces south, capturing Damascus, Tyre, Gaza, and Egypt. In 331 BC he marched to Mesopotamia for his third, and final, battle with the Persians. This battle took place at Gaugamela, just east of the Tigris River near the ancient city of Nineveh. Darius fled, and Alexander took over most of the remaining Persian Empire.

Alexander returned from his Asian conquest and settled temporarily at Babylon. He died there in 323 BC at the age of thirty-three. Over the next fifty years his empire was divided among four generals. Seleucus controlled Persia, Babylonia, and eastern Asia Minor. Ptolemy gained control of Egypt and most of Canaan. Cassander ruled over Macedonia and most of Greece, and Lysimachus controlled Thrace and the western edge of Asia Minor.

The Roman Period

Rome extended its influence eastward in 169 BC when a Roman naval fleet thwarted Antiochus IV's attack on Egypt. This event, predicted in Daniel 11:29–30, expanded Rome's control eastward. When King Attalus III of Pergamum willed his territory to the Romans in 133 BC, Rome also gained control over much of western Asia Minor.

The Romans attached great importance to Asia Minor, and Asia Minor appreciated Rome. In some areas of Asia Minor, the Roman emperors were better known than they were back in Rome. Roman architecture and Roman fashion permeated the region. Cities constructed magnificent Roman baths with frigidarium (cold baths), tepidarium (warm baths), and caldarium (steam rooms). They constructed Roman-style aqueducts to supply these ever-expanding cities with a sufficient supply of clean water, and they connected the cities with Roman roads.

The Seven Churches of Revelation 2–3

NAME	CHARACTERISTIC	DESCRIPTION OF CHRIST	PROMISE
Ephesus	Loveless (Dead orthodoxy)	He is present He is controlling	Eternal life
Smyrna	Persecuted	He has risen from the dead	No second death
Pergamum	Compromising—Morally & doctrinally	He has a word of judgment	Christ will be sufficient for their needs
Thyatira	Tolerant of sin	He can see all that happens	Authority to rule the world
Sardis	Dead spiritually	He has the life-giving Holy Spirit	Assurance of eternal life
Philadelphia	Faithful	He has the authority	Honored position with God
Laodicea	Lukewarm	His is a truthful ruler	Fellowship and rulership with Christ

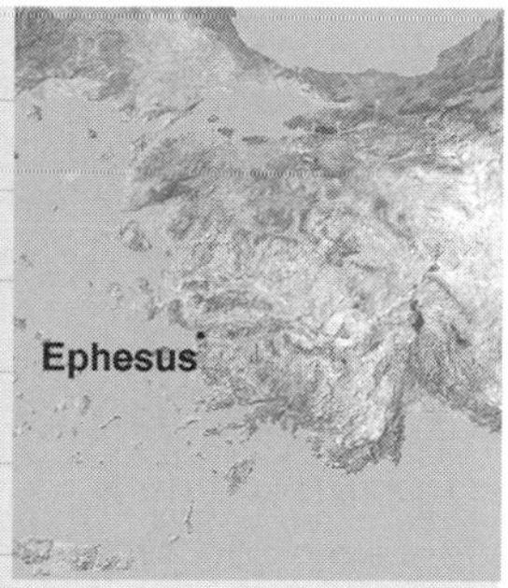

EPHESUS

Ephesus was an important seaport city in the Roman province of Asia. The city was also located at the intersection of two major overland routes—the coastal road that ran north through Smyrna and Pergamum to Troas, and the road that ran east to Colossae, Laodicea, and the interior of Asia Minor. This strategic location made Ephesus a major commercial and religious center. The temple of Artemis (Diana) was known throughout the Mediterranean area, and thousands of pilgrims flocked to Ephesus during the festivals of Artemis. Herodotus identified this temple as one of the seven wonders of the ancient world.

Inside the temple was a statue of Artemis (Diana) that was at least partially fashioned from a meteorite. This explains the statement of the city clerk in Ephesus in Acts 19:35: "Men of Ephesus, doesn't all the world know that the city of Ephesus is the guardian of the temple of the great Artemis and of her image, which fell from heaven?" During the time of the New Testament, the city likely had a population in excess of 250,000. The city theater could seat twenty-five thousand.

Statue of the goddess Artemis/Diana, whose temple was a major religious center in Ephesus

Apostolic Age *Acts 18:19–28*— Paul stopped briefly in Ephesus on his return to Jerusalem at the end of his second missionary journey. Paul left Priscilla and

Aquila behind in Ephesus while he returned to Jerusalem. Later, Priscilla and Aquila discipled Apollos in Ephesus before Apollos went on to Achaia (and Corinth).

Acts 19:1–20:1—Paul went to Ephesus on his third missionary journey and stayed there for nearly three years. He spoke in the Jewish synagogue for three months and then had daily discussions in the lecture hall of Tyrannus. Paul's time in Ephesus ended following a riot incited by the silversmiths.

Acts 20:16–38—On his return to Jerusalem at the end of his third missionary journey, Paul decided against stopping in Ephesus. But while in Miletus he called for the elders of the church at Ephesus and warned them against false teachers who would try to slip in among them.

Theater of Ephesus where the silversmiths rioted against the apostl

Ephesians—While imprisoned for the first time in Rome, Paul wrote his letter to the Ephesians. The date of this letter is approximately AD 60. The letter was probably intended both for the church at Ephesus and for the churches in the surrounding area.

After Paul's release from his first Roman imprisonment, he evidently returned to Ephesus about AD 65–66 as part of his further travels. Paul's earlier warning to the elders concerning false teachers must have come true, and Paul left Timothy in Ephesus to "command certain men not to teach false doctrines any longer" (1 Tim. 1:3). Shortly after leaving Ephesus and heading to Nicopolis, Paul was arrested, taken to Rome, tried, and beheaded.

Tradition says the apostle John settled in Ephesus and had a profound impact on the city. During the reign of Domitian, John was exiled from Ephesus to the island of Patmos. It was there that he wrote the book of Revelation about AD 95. The first of the seven letters to the churches written in Revelation was addressed to the church at Ephesus (Rev. 2:1–7).

LAODICEA

Laodicea sat at the crossroads of north–south traffic between Sardis and Pergamum, and east–west traffic from the Euphrates to Ephesus. As a result, it quickly became a wealthy city. The origins of the city stretch back into the third century BC, and the city is thought to have been named in honor of King Antiochus II's wife, Laodicea.

The Laodiceans produced an eye salve that was recognized for its therapeutic powers. Galen described this salve as something that was "made best only in Laodicea in Asia." The city was also located in a region well suited for raising sheep. Their black wool produced excellent revenue for the town. Laodicea was also known for its textile industry and produced a special type of cloth that came to be called Laodicean, as well as a style of tunic called trimita. This tunic was so popular throughout the ancient world that Laodicea was nicknamed Trimitaria.

The one great problem with Laodicea was its lack of a water supply. Its water had to be brought by aqueduct for a distance of five miles. Six miles away were the warm springs of Hierapolis, unsuitable for drinking but famous for their therapeutic qualities.

Apostolic Age *Colossians 4:13*—Christianity probably came to Laodicea as a result of Paul's ministry in Ephesus; it appears that Paul never visited Laodicea.

Revelation 3:14–22—Laodicea was the self-sufficient church that thought it was rich but was, in reality, "wretched, pitiful, poor, blind and naked."

PERGAMUM/BERGAMA

Pergamum was an ancient city in northwest Asia Minor, in the region of Mysia. It later became the capital of the kingdom of Pergamum. The acropolis of Pergamum looks down majestically on the rest of the city.

What remains of the city is largely from the Hellenistic and Roman periods. Lysimachus, a general under Alexander the Great, brought prominence to the city when he chose it as a stronghold for his treasures. Attalus I Soter (241–197 BC) made Pergamum a great center of art and culture. Pergamum became the rival of Ephesus in the field of commerce, and of Alexandria in the fields of learning and arts.

Pergamum was the city that invented parchment after Egypt cut off its supply of papyrus. Parchment was made from untanned animal skins, especially the skins of sheep, calves, and goats. The skins were soaked, scraped, and stretched, then rubbed with chalk and pumice. The final product was far more durable than papyrus. The English word "parchment" is derived from the name *pergamene*, the name given to this leather.

Remains of the temple dedicated to Emperor Trajan

The city's prosperity and power continued under Attalus II Philadelphus (ca. 160–138 BC) and Attalus III Philometor (138–133 BC). At his death, Attalus III bequeathed his kingdom to the Romans because he lacked an heir to his throne. During his reign, the population of the city grew to approximately 140,000 people.

The ancient city of Pergamum was noted for two things: its library and its temple to Zeus. The library was the second largest in the world.

Apostolic Age *Revelation 2:12–17*—Pergamum was a church holding fast to Christ, even though they lived "where Satan has his throne" (cf. Rev. 2:13). Unfortunately, some in the church were being seduced into compromising their faith.

PHILADELPHIA/ALASEHIR

Philadelphia, today known as Alasehir, is about seventy-five miles east of Smyrna (Izmir) and twenty-eight miles southeast of Sardis. The geographical location of the city was very important: on a high hill overlooking the Persian Royal Road and two important valleys. The city was in a grape-growing region. As a result, the most respected god was Dionysus, the god of wine.

The word Philadelphia means "brotherly love," and the city of Philadelphia was founded by Attalus II Philadelphus, king of Pergamum. He was given the title of Philadelphus because of his love for his brother Eumenes, who was the previous king of Pergamum. By AD 19 Greek had completely replaced the native Lydian dialect as the common language of the city.

Philadelphia suffered repeatedly from earthquakes, so much so that even the city walls had been broken. Strabo wrote, "The city Philadelphia [is] ever subject to earthquakes. Incessantly the walls of the houses are cracked, different parts of the city being thus affected at different times."

Apostolic Age *Revelation 3:7–13*—
Philadelphia was the church that received God's highest commendation. He promised to keep them from the "hour of trial" He would bring upon the whole world.

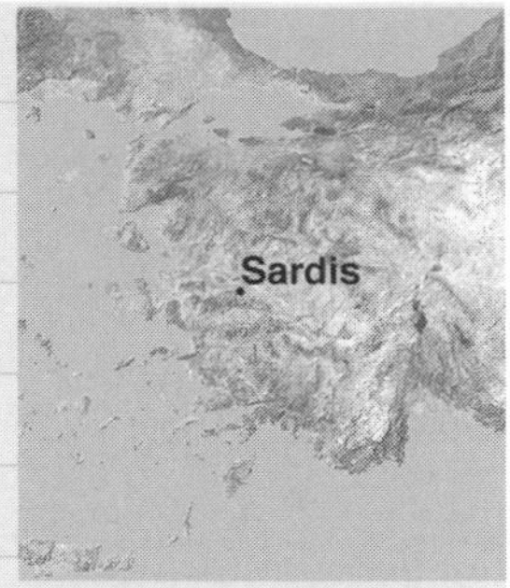

SARDIS/SART

The site of the ancient Lydian capital of Sardis is located near the present-day village of Sart. Sardis was the capital of the famous kingdom of Lydia in western Asia Minor.

The last king of the Lydian Empire was Croesus, whose wealth gave rise to the expression "as rich as Croesus." Croesus extended his kingdom through conquests in western Asia Minor. But when he invaded Cappadocia (now in eastern Turkey), the Persian army led by Cyrus the Great conquered Croesus; his empire fell to the Persians in 546 BC.

Sardis was conquered by Alexander the Great in the fourth century BC, and by the second century BC it had come under Roman control.

Temple of Artemis with the Acropolis of Sardis in the backgrou

Divided Kingdom *Obadiah 20*—In the ninth century BC the prophet Obadiah told of Israelites being carried away by the Phoenicians to be sold as slaves in "Sepharad." The spelling of this word in Hebrew has led many scholars to conclude that Obadiah was referring to Sardis.

Apostolic Age *Revelation 3:1–6*—Sardis was the church with a reputation for being alive, but God announced that it was dead.

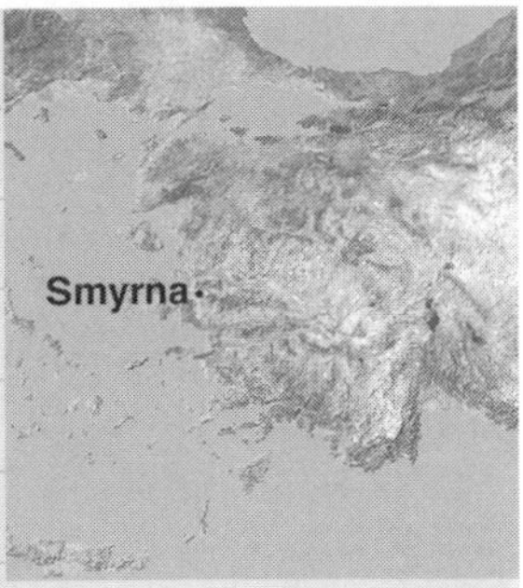

SMYRNA/IZMIR

The modern city of Izmir lies below the hill known in antiquity as Mount Pagus, the acropolis of the ancient city. Izmir/Smyrna lies at the head of a long, narrow gulf and is Turkey's second most important port. The famous Greek geographer Strabo recorded the popular belief that the cities of Smyrna and Ephesus were founded by the Amazons, a legendary race of women warriors.

The original city was established in the third millennium BC. By 1500 BC it was part of the Hittite Empire. Later, it ranked as one of the important cities of the Ionian Federation in western Asia Minor. Homer is thought to have lived

Agora of ancient Smyrna, in the modern Turkish coastal city of Iz

in Smyrna during this time. The Lydian conquest of the city, about 600 BC, brought Smyrna's first period of greatness to an end. In the fourth century BC Alexander the Great encouraged the building of a new city in this location.

The Roman period, from the first century BC, gave birth to Smyrna's second great era. While the Romans sacked the city to capture one of the assassins of Julius Caesar who had taken refuge there, they later gave the city permission to build a temple to Augustus and his mother. Smyrna became a prosperous port connecting the Aegean Sea with the wealth of Asia Minor.

The famous early church leader Polycarp served as bishop of Smyrna from AD 115 to 156. He and eleven other Christians from Philadelphia were burned at the stake in 156 during a period of persecution.

Apostolic Age *Revelation 2:8–11*—Smyrna was the poor, persecuted church that God announced was rich.

THYATIRA/AKHISAR

Thyatira was founded by the Lydians and was called Pelopia. Seleucus I Nicator ("conqueror"), one of Alexander the Great's generals, took control of the city in the third century BC and changed its name to Thyatira. The city was located in a broad valley and was a center of commerce and trade.

In 190 BC Thyatira came under the control of Pergamum. When the king of Pergamum died in 133 BC, he bequeathed his kingdom, including Thyatira, to the Romans because he lacked an heir to his throne.

Thyatira was known throughout the ancient world for its well-developed trade and manufacturing guilds that specialized in the production of bread, pottery, bronze, leather goods, wool, and linen. Membership in such guilds was probably essential for employment, but this caused problems for believers, because membership also involved participating in immoral, pagan religious practices and attending banquets where food had been sacrificed to idols. Thyatira was also known for its production of "purple" (Turkish red) dye that came from the madder root rather than from shellfish. This dye was highly prized, and the Thyatirans exported purple cloth throughout the region.

Apostolic Age *Acts 16:14*—When Paul arrived in Philippi, his first convert was "Lydia, a dealer in purple cloth from the city of Thyatira."

Revelation 2:18–29—Thyatira was a church condemned by Christ for tolerating the teaching of a woman (called "Jezebel") who encouraged the believers to give in to immorality and idolatry.

PART SEVEN

Preserving Your Trip

- My Photos
- Tour Notes

MY PHOTOS

Location/Description:	Location/Description:
1	1
2	2
3	3
4	4
5	5
6	6
7	7
8	8
9	9
10	10
11	11
12	12
13	13
14	14
15	15
16	16
17	17
18	18
19	19
20	20
21	21
22	22
23	23
24	24
25	25
26	26
27	27
28	28
29	29
30	30
31	31
32	32
33	33
34	34
35	35
36	36

MY PHOTOS

Location/Description:	Location/Description:
1	1
2	2
3	3
4	4
5	5
6	6
7	7
8	8
9	9
10	10
11	11
12	12
13	13
14	14
15	15
16	16
17	17
18	18
19	19
20	20
21	21
22	22
23	23
24	24
25	25
26	26
27	27
28	28
29	29
30	30
31	31
32	32
33	33
34	34
35	35
36	36

MY PHOTOS

Location/Description:	Location/Description:
1	1
2	2
3	3
4	4
5	5
6	6
7	7
8	8
9	9
10	10
11	11
12	12
13	13
14	14
15	15
16	16
17	17
18	18
19	19
20	20
21	21
22	22
23	23
24	24
25	25
26	26
27	27
28	28
29	29
30	30
31	31
32	32
33	33
34	34
35	35
36	36

MY PHOTOS

Location/Description:	Location/Description:
1	1
2	2
3	3
4	4
5	5
6	6
7	7
8	8
9	9
10	10
11	11
12	12
13	13
14	14
15	15
16	16
17	17
18	18
19	19
20	20
21	21
22	22
23	23
24	24
25	25
26	26
27	27
28	28
29	29
30	30
31	31
32	32
33	33
34	34
35	35
36	36

TOUR NOTES

TOUR NOTES

TOUR NOTES

TOUR NOTES

Other Resources from Charles Dyer

- *Storm Clouds on the Horizon,* Charles H. Dyer, general editor
  Dr. Dyer and members of the Moody Bible Institute faculty help you understand what biblical prophecies reveal about events in the Holy Land today. Dyer wrote the chapter, "Jerusalem: Eye of the Storm," to explain how the city of David remains important to Jews, Muslims, and Christians. ISBN: **978-0-8024-0948-5**

- *A Voice in the Wilderness,* by Charles H. Dyer
  In this powerful study of Isaiah 40 and personal adversity, Dr. Dyer draws our attention to the compassionate, powerful Lord who cares for His people. The book includes eight "postcards from the wilderness," personal stories of men and women who have suffered, and found comfort in the Lord and answers to their prayers. **ISBN: 978-0-8024-2908-7**

- *What's Next?* by Charles H. Dyer
  Although Saddam Hussein has been captured, tried, and executed, the war in Iraq continues. Dyer brings Bible prophecy alive as he looks at past and present Arab-Israeli conflict, and the role of Iraq and its ancient city Babylon, in future Middle East events. **ISBN: 978-0-8024-0907-2**

- *Strike the Dragon,* by Charles H. Dyer and Mark Tobey
  In this international thriller, Bible professor Greg Hanson discovers a cryptic message on a Web site. Yet it may be too late to stop the chain of events leading to a terrorist attack on U.S. soil. Special agents and covert operatives track clues to pinpoint the location of an enemy who intends to strike at the heart of U.S. commerce and transportation. **ISBN: 978-0-8024-3908-6**